THE CHURCH MOVES OUT

A Devotional Commentary on the Catholic Epistles

GENERAL EDITOR

Leo Zanchettin

The Word Among Us Press
9639 Doctor Perry Road
Ijamsville, Maryland 21754
www.wordamongus.org

10 09 08 07 06 1 2 3 4 5

ISBN 10: 1-59325-082-7
ISBN 13: 978-1-59325-082-9

Cover design by David Crosson

Cover image: Harbor of Classe. Early Christian mosaic. 6th CE.
Location: S. Apollinare Nuovo, Ravenna, Italy
Photo Credit: Scala / Art Resource, NY

Made and printed in the United States of America

Library of Congress Control Number: 2006925935

Table of Contents

Acknowledgments

I want to thank everyone who has made this commentary possible, especially all of the writers who contributed meditations. Some of the meditations appearing in this book were initially developed for *The Word Among Us* monthly publication, and I am grateful to these writers for granting us permission to reprint their work. I also want to thank Steve Binz, Fr. Jude Winkler, OFM Conv, Fr. Henry Wansbrough, OSB, Fr. Joseph Mindling, OFM Cap, and Fr. Joseph Wimmer, OSA, for contributing the chapters introducing the various letters in this commentary. A special note of thanks also goes to Jill Boughton, Barry Burrus, Bob French, and Hallie Riedel for their considerable contributions to the meditations. Thanks, too, go to Margaret Procario for her keen eye and sound ear in editing the manuscript, and to Kathy Mayne for all the work she did in gathering and collating much of the material that went into this book. Finally, I want to thank Patricia Mitchell, editor of The Word Among Us Press, whose gentle prodding kept me going when other projects threatened this one. May the Lord abundantly bless each of them!

Leo Zanchettin
Editor, *The Word Among Us*

Introduction

How Did the Church Ever Make It to the Second Century?

Leo Zanchettin

What do you do when your church is rocked by scandal, or when some members of your parish are stirring up strife and dissension? Where do you turn when "the way things used to be" in the church seems upended, and you're left wondering how you should live as a Christian now?

Whether it is the changes introduced at Vatican II, the sexual-abuse scandal of the past decade, or some other problem in our parish or diocese, we have all learned that life in the church is not always easy. We are, after all, a gathering of sinners, each with his or her own unique combination of strengths, weaknesses, quirks, and pitfalls. Why, then, should we expect everything to always run smoothly? Of course there will be difficulties and mistakes. Of course people will get hurt from time to time. Human nature being what it is, we couldn't expect anything different!

How Did They Do It? And things haven't changed much in the last two millennia. The second-generation Christians to whom the epistles in this commentary were addressed faced changes and disturbances as the early church moved out of the comfortable familiarity of its founding years and into the larger world a generation later. No longer could believers rally around the heroes of its first decades. No longer could they rely upon firsthand witnesses to Jesus' teaching or his resurrection. For the most part, those heroes were dead, and a new crop of disciples was left to carry on their work.

From the general trials and sufferings faced by the people addressed in 1 Peter to the specific challenge posed by heretical teachers in the Letter of Jude, we see communities wondering how they will ever be able to keep themselves together and preserve the heritage of the gospel as the apostles handed it down. Likewise, in the communities addressed in the Letter of James and in 1 John, we see churches slowly dividing, whether from personality clashes or from internal disagreements over questions of doctrine. How could these churches continue to shine out to the world as witnesses to the power of the gospel when it seemed that they could not even stay together themselves?

When we think about the early church in this light, we might wonder how this next generation of disciples was able to survive at all, let alone attract any new converts to the faith. We might even ask what we can learn from them as we try to tackle our own challenges, both as individual believers and as members of the larger body of Christ. If they could survive, and even thrive, shouldn't we be able to do the same? What was their secret?

Three Simple Words. There are probably countless ways to answer this question, but in the end, every one of those answers can be boiled down into three simple words: love one another!

It may sound trite or clichéd, but the conviction that underlies all seven of these letters is the belief that love can cover "a multitude of sins" (1 Peter 4:8). It is the reason why James urges his readers to treat one another with the same love that God has for them—rich and poor, powerful and unassuming alike (James 2:1-7). It is why the author of 1 John told his readers that if they loved one another, they would remain safe "in the light" (1 John 2:10), and not be subject to the darkness around them. And it is the reason why Jude calls his audience to have mercy upon one another, especially those whose faith is wavering (Jude 22). For all of these writers, as well as for the people in their churches, mutual love had the power to beat back the forces that threatened their unity and their survival—both the major challenges like heresy and serious sin as well as the smaller challenges we all face, such as judgmental attitudes and petty suspicions.

Why all this focus on love? Why not reassert the doctrines of the gospel more forcefully so that everyone will conform to the truth? Why not insist that those who are wavering simply leave so that the church might be freed of all of its dead weight? Because it is in the commitment to love one another that the Holy Spirit is the most free to strengthen the church and bring others to conversion. Let's face it: unconditional love—loving one another "deeply from the heart" (1 Peter 1:22)—is the hardest thing we could ever do. It's the one commitment we make that is sure to bring us to the end of our own human abilities. And that's precisely where we should end up. How else will we learn to surrender our cherished opinions and judgments to the Lord and let him teach us *his* way to love? How else will we learn to become vessels of divine power and divine love—the power and love that can transform our lives as well as the lives of those around us?

This is the kind of love that kept the next generations of Christians together and preserved the church. This is the kind of love that empowered these believers—weak and wounded though they may have felt at times—to continue evangelizing. This is the kind of love that allowed the early Christians to continue performing miracles, both within their congregations and as they went out to do the work of the kingdom.

It is our hope and prayer that the meditations in this volume reflect the same love that kept these early believers together: both the love of a God who would offer up his only Son for us and the love that all believers are privileged to share with one another. So whatever you learn as you read and pray through this book, may you come to a deeper and more exciting experience of love. May that love give you a new perspective on problems in the church in our own day. And may that love compel you to move out into the world with the saving, powerful, loving message of the gospel.

Live Out Your Faith!

The Letter of James

LIVE OUT YOUR FAITH

Live Out Your Faith!
An Introduction to the Letter of James

Stephen J. Binz

Unlike most of St. Paul's letters, which begin with a presentation of doctrine and end with a series of exhortations, the Letter of James has been described as a work of exhortation from beginning to end. In virtually every chapter, James urges us to "walk the walk," to express our belief in Jesus Christ through the way we live our daily lives. James leaves no room for equivocation or fence-straddling. His writing is vibrant and vivid, filled with rhetorical questions, exclamations, and practical examples as he urges us to examine the way we live and to choose to live fully for Christ. In fact, if you want to capture more fully the challenge presented by this letter, read it aloud, just as its first recipients read it. You'll be amazed at how much more of the letter resonates in your ears and echoes in your heart.

James' overarching concern is that our Christian faith go beyond the abstract and speculative. It must be concrete and embedded in every aspect of our lives. The word of God that has been planted in us must make a difference in the way we live every day. "Be doers of the word," James urges, "and not merely hearers" (James 1:22). We can have a great deal of intellectual knowledge about the teachings of Jesus and the apostles, but if we only *hear* the word and not *do* the word, we deceive ourselves. Of course, knowledge is the important foundation for action, but it is our obedience to the word that ultimately matters.

Like the wisdom literature of the Old Testament, James contrasts two different ways to live: that of the world and that of God. Like Paul, James used the term "the world" not to designate material, bodily reality but to refer to all that is opposed to God's will and purpose (James 4:4). The way of the world, then, is a system of values in which everyone is in competition and envious of one another. One person's gain is another's loss. The way of God, in contrast, is a system of values that sees everything, even life itself, as a divine gift. Since God has given us all that we have and all that we are, we are able to live as God lives, "generously and ungrudgingly" (1:5). This alternative way of life is distinguished by works "done with gentleness born of wisdom" (3:13). The false wisdom of the world is characterized by envy, selfish ambition, and boastfulness, but "the wisdom from above is first pure, then peaceable, gentle, willing to yield, full of mercy and good fruits, without a trace of partiality or hypocrisy" (3:17).

Who Was James? James (Jacob is the Hebrew equivalent) was a common name in the Jewish world of the first century. Two of Jesus' twelve disciples are named James. But the James who is traditionally considered the author of this letter is the James who is often called "brother of the Lord" (Matthew 13:55; Mark 6:3), probably a close relative or cousin of Jesus. Though this James did not follow Jesus during his lifetime, Paul tells us that the risen Lord appeared to him. And like the appearance to Paul, this was probably an experience of conversion (1 Corinthians 15:7).

James introduces himself in his letter as "servant of God and of the Lord Jesus Christ" (James 1:1). He became the leader of the Jewish Christian community in Jerusalem, and Paul acknowledged him, along with Peter and John, as one of the "pillars" of the church (Galatians 2:9). In the Acts of the Apostles, James is shown to be the spokesman for the Jewish Christians who presided over the apostolic council held in Jerusalem (Acts 15:13-21). According to the Jewish historian Josephus, he was stoned to death under the high priest Ananias II in A.D. 62. Just four years later, the Jewish

Christian community in Jerusalem scattered in fear of the advancing Roman armies.

The primary argument against James' authorship of this letter is its fine Greek language and style. Would a Palestinian Jew, who wrote in Hebrew and Aramaic, have been able to produce such a letter? It is probable that James acted more as the authority behind the letter rather than as its actual writer—a common approach in ancient literature. James was probably the primary source of the sayings in the letter, and the letter most likely expresses his central teachings. But a Jew immersed in Greek culture and comfortable with the Greek language probably collected James' teachings and expressed them in the form of a letter, either shortly before or shortly after James' death. Just as Paul had a secretary or disciple to write many of his letters, and just as Luke improved the Greek of many of Jesus' sayings, so the writer of this letter preserved the teachings of James in Greek for future generations.

The fact that James was from the family of Jesus in Galilee and head of the church in Jerusalem put him in an ideal position to remember and preserve the teachings of Jesus. Readers who are familiar with the gospels will recognize that the themes presented in James are very close to the words of Jesus, especially the ethical teachings recorded in the Sermon on the Mount (Matthew 5–7) and the Sermon on the Plain (Luke 6). In fact, forty-six of the one hundred eight verses of the letter echo the teachings of Jesus as they are recorded in the gospels. Though James never quotes Jesus directly in the letter, there is no other New Testament writing outside the gospels with so many echoes of the voice of Jesus.

The early Christians learned the teachings of Jesus by heart, just as other Jews of the time memorized the words of their favorite rabbis. These teachings were the rule of life for the early communities. When James alluded to the teachings of Jesus, he realized that Christians would recognize that Jesus was the source of his words. With this realization, we can also speculate that many of the other sayings and proverbs in this letter also came from the teachings of Jesus. After all, it's unlikely that the gospels recorded everything that Jesus taught, and few people were in a better position to preserve his additional teachings than James.

Thus, the Letter of James is a wonderful example of how the early Christians used Jesus' words and applied them to their daily lives. And in this lies the challenge to Christians in every age. The letter serves as an authoritative model for us of how to draw on the teachings of Jesus to address contemporary issues.

The Community and Teachings of James. The social and religious setting of the church in Jerusalem, with James as its leader, seems to be the context of this letter. The Jewish Christians continued to live as Jews, praying together in the form of a synagogue liturgy, followed by the celebration of the Lord's Supper. They met in a series of house churches, each with its own elders, presided over by James. The Jewish Christians also continued to celebrate the Jewish feasts and the temple services.

The church in Jerusalem was predominantly poor, especially compared to the more economically diversified gentile churches to which Paul ministered. Though many wealthy and influential Jews joined the Christian community, the teachings of the church appealed mostly to poor and oppressed people—the same people who were attracted to Jesus. Within much of Jewish society, the Christians were a despised sect, often suffering from economic persecution. The church offered hospitality in the form of food and housing for those who came to Jerusalem to join this sect, which only served to increase the church's material needs.

Given this context, we can see why James presents a theology of suffering in the midst of a church undergoing trial. Though the church is pressured to compromise with the world, James urges Christians to endure their afflictions patiently and even joyfully. He teaches that God has "chosen the poor in the world to be rich in faith and to be heirs of the kingdom that he has promised to those who love him" (James 2:5). Standing faithfully in the midst of trial requires that Christians trust in God without reservation. They must refuse to put their hope in the world and its false securities. Instead they are to pray—not for the things of the world, which only rust and decay—but for divine wisdom to live as God wills "until the coming of the Lord" (5:7).

A Checkered History. Though the Letter of James is often a favorite among people today who are concerned with the practical implications of Christianity, it was not always looked upon so favorably. In fact, several times in history this letter was almost excluded from the canon of the New Testament.

In the early church, the four gospels and the letters of Paul were the first to be incorporated into the liturgy and considered as sacred writings. The earliest list of New Testament books, the famous Muratorian Canon (from about A.D. 160), does not include Hebrews, the letters of James and Peter, or the Third Letter of John. For the first few centuries, James was often not included in the lists of inspired books. It took the authority of Sts. Jerome and Augustine to dispel the doubts and ensure the Letter of James a place in the inspired literature of the church.

The biblical status of James' letter remained uncontested until the sixteenth century, when Martin Luther described it as "an epistle of straw." In his preface to James, Luther wrote, "In the first place, it is flatly against St. Paul and all the rest of Scripture in ascribing justification to works. . . . In the second place, its purpose is to teach Christians, but in all this long teaching it does not once mention the Passion, the Resurrection, or the Spirit of Christ." For Luther, this was a decisive argument against the letter's apostolic authority.

After Luther's death, the Lutheran Church and all the churches of the Protestant Reformation accepted the Letter of James as part of the New Testament. For Catholics, the Council of Trent solemnly reaffirmed the Letter of James along with all the other New Testament writings as the canon of inspired Scripture for the whole church. As a sacred book of Scripture, James must be heard and honored, in the same way that the gospels and Paul's letters are revered.

Saved by Grace. Luther saw an apparent conflict between the teachings of Paul—"We hold that a person is justified by faith apart from works prescribed by the law" (Romans 3:28)—and the teachings of James—"A person is justified by works and not by faith alone" (James 2:24). But modern scholars show that there is no direct contradiction here, only a difference in the two writers' use of the word "works." Paul is addressing non-Jews, telling them that they do not need to perform all the "works prescribed by the law," like circumcision and dietary laws, in order to receive the salvation offered by Jesus. On the other hand, James is addressing Jewish Christians, telling them that charitable works toward those in need are essential accompaniments to Christian faith.

James is well aware that we are saved by God's grace, not because of anything we have done to earn it (James 1:17-18, 21). Likewise, Paul is well aware that works of love are a vital part of our response to God's grace. James and Paul express different aspects of our saving relationship with God, and we are richer for having both of their insights.

Although James was criticized for not proclaiming the heart of Christianity—the death and resurrection of Christ—his letter is an outstanding example of the way early Christians applied the teachings of Jesus to communal life. He focuses on the practical issues of how to live the Christian life in the midst of the world, insisting that we bridge the gap between what we say we believe and what we actually do.

Controversy—or Challenge? As a work of exhortation, the writing of James is strongly Jewish in character. It echoes the prophets of Israel in its denunciation of both social injustice and neglect of the poor. It also shares a similar style with the wisdom writings of the Old Testament, especially Sirach, in the way it urges its readers toward practical means of choosing the way of God and rejecting the ways of the world.

We would expect such a challenging work to be controversial. The Christian life, when lived authentically, has never been clear or easy. So let's read this exhortation of James expecting to be challenged, so that we may always be "doers of the word" (James 1:22).

LIVE OUT YOUR FAITH

James 1:1-11

¹ James, a servant of God and of the Lord Jesus Christ,
To the twelve tribes in the Dispersion:
Greetings.

² My brothers and sisters, whenever you face trials of any kind, consider it nothing but joy, ³because you know that the testing of your faith produces endurance; ⁴and let endurance have its full effect, so that you may be mature and complete, lacking in nothing.

⁵ If any of you is lacking in wisdom, ask God, who gives to all generously and ungrudgingly, and it will be given you. ⁶But ask in faith, never doubting, for the one who doubts is like a wave of the sea, driven and tossed by the wind; ⁷,⁸for the doubter, being double-minded and unstable in every way, must not expect to receive anything from the Lord.

⁹ Let the believer who is lowly boast in being raised up, ¹⁰and the rich in being brought low, because the rich will disappear like a flower in the field. ¹¹For the sun rises with its scorching heat and withers the field; its flower falls, and its beauty perishes. It is the same way with the rich; in the midst of a busy life, they will wither away.

Can't we all just get along? The answer for James, as he looked at the church, was yes—but only with a deeper understanding of Jesus.

James encouraged both the rich and the poor in his church to take pride only in the fact that they are now incorporated into the body of Christ. For in the body of Christ a unity exists that encompasses many diversities. Once we are baptized into Christ Jesus, we are a new creation; old divisions no longer apply. God shows no partiality, and so there is no distinction whatsoever between rich and poor, male and female, gentile and Jew (Galatians 3:28). In Jesus, we are one. If Jesus could turn a tax collector, a political activist, a few simple tradesmen, and a well-educated Pharisee into a strong apostolic brotherhood, he can unite all of us, as well.

Jesus taught that life is more than external things such as food, clothing, and shelter (Matthew 6:25-33). Though wealth may seem to be desirable, the only thing that truly satisfies is a relationship with the Lord. James reminded those under his care that, in the end, poverty and wealth come out even. The rich will not fare any better than the poor in the life to come, so it makes no sense to allow such distinctions to divide the church now (James 2:1-13). Quite often, God acts to humble the rich and raise up the poor in order to teach everyone to rely on him alone and not seek satisfaction in the things of this world.

Rich and poor alike must strive for an equality of love and honor among all of God's people. As Christians, we should be the last people to put others in boxes according to the size of their bank accounts. Instead, let us learn to recognize the true beauty that is in each person because of the presence of Christ. When we see Christ in one another, we will be able to live as the one body of Christ and experience what it means to be the family of God.

"Lord Jesus, help me to perceive the true value of each person, rich or poor. Bring unity to your body, so that we will be one, as you are one with your Father. Make us visibly your family, so that the world will believe that you are with us."

James 1:12-18

[12] Blessed is anyone who endures temptation. Such a one has stood the test and will receive the crown of life that the Lord has prom-

ised to those who love him. ¹³No one, when tempted, should say, "I am being tempted by God"; for God cannot be tempted by evil and he himself tempts no one. ¹⁴But one is tempted by one's own desire, being lured and enticed by it; ¹⁵then, when that desire has conceived, it gives birth to sin, and that sin, when it is fully grown, gives birth to death. ¹⁶Do not be deceived, my beloved.

¹⁷ Every generous act of giving, with every perfect gift, is from above, coming down from the Father of lights, with whom there is no variation or shadow due to change. ¹⁸In fulfillment of his own purpose he gave us birth by the word of truth, so that we would become a kind of first fruits of his creatures.

To know God truly is to know that he is all loving, all good, all merciful, and that no evil dwells in him. To know ourselves truly is to know that we are sinners, one and all. This is a painful fact, which we often prefer to minimize. Like our first parents, we tend to place the blame for our sins elsewhere—either on another person or on our general circumstances.

How easy it is to see the good we do and the wrong others do! By contrast, it is utter grace to take responsibility for our condition. We need God's help to overcome our tendency to avoid coping with life's trials and temptations.

God created us for friendship with himself. His central desire is that we would all come to share in his holiness through a life of surrender to Jesus Christ. He sees the potential in us to be good, loving, and merciful, but he also sees our sins—more clearly than we do. God knows exactly what stands in the way of our becoming the men and women he created us to be. He knows how difficult our struggle against sin is (Romans 7:13-25). And he has provided everything we need to break free from sin. In a supreme act of love, Jesus redeemed us from sin by willingly sacrificing his life on the cross. By union with Jesus through baptism and faith, God fills each of us with his own life and enables us to lead a life free from sin and pleasing to him.

Don't be afraid to examine yourself honestly and acknowledge your sin. Let God shine into your darkened heart—not just to expose your sin, but to remove it. The most balanced, hopeful people in the world are those who know both the darkness in their hearts and the gift of the Holy Spirit that comes from the Father of lights. God is the giver of every good and perfect gift. Let's allow him to free us from darkness so that we can become the light of Christ to everyone we meet.

"O Lord, you know when I sit and when I stand. You are acquainted with all my ways. Search me, O God, and know my heart! Try me and know my thoughts! See if there are hurtful ways in me, and lead me in the way everlasting."

James 1:19-27

[19] You must understand this, my beloved: let everyone be quick to listen, slow to speak, slow to anger; [20]for your anger does not produce God's righteousness. [21]Therefore rid yourselves of all sordidness and rank growth of wickedness, and welcome with meekness the implanted word that has the power to save your souls.

[22] But be doers of the word, and not merely hearers who deceive themselves. [23]For if any are hearers of the word and not doers, they are like those who look at themselves in a mirror; [24]for they look at themselves and, on going away, immediately forget what they were like. [25]But those who look into the perfect law, the law of liberty, and persevere, being not hearers who forget but doers who act—they will be blessed in their doing.

²⁶ If any think they are religious, and do not bridle their tongues but deceive their hearts, their religion is worthless. ²⁷Religion that is pure and undefiled before God, the Father, is this: to care for orphans and widows in their distress, and to keep oneself unstained by the world. ✑

How do we become "doers of the word" (James 1:22)? By yielding to the transforming presence of Christ in us. As we do, our everyday actions will give outward expression to the inner reality of God's presence in our hearts.

For example, Rabbi Eugenio Zolli converted to the Catholic Church because he witnessed the faith of its leader. As chief rabbi in Rome during World War II, Zolli was a hunted man. He credited Pope Pius XII for saving his life, the lives of his family, and the lives of hundreds of Jews by helping them elude Nazi persecutors. The Vatican's secret charity moved Zolli to embrace baptism in 1945.

Dorothy Day, a popular Catholic social activist, described the influence of her unassuming Catholic roommate in nursing school. Though Day was an agnostic at the time, the witness of her friend's quiet, regular devotions left a lasting impression on her: "I came to admire her greatly and to associate all her natural goodness and ability with Catholicism. . . . [Her] faith was so solid a part of her life that she didn't need to talk about it. I felt the healthiness of her soul [and] I began to go to Mass with her on Sunday" (*From Union Square to Rome*, on the Internet at www.catholic.org). Years later, Day herself became a Catholic and devoted her life to loving and caring for the poor and needy.

We never know the effects that a "normal" life in the Spirit will produce. On an Internet forum about conversion, a secretary wrote that she was led to a deeper faith experience through the quiet strength and dignity of her boss and his wife as he fought a protracted and ultimately unsuccessful battle with cancer. The man's simple life and death in Christ were a more eloquent witness than hours of lectures might have been.

The indwelling Christ can accomplish so much in a surrendered heart. He empowers us to respond naturally, with humility, whenever we are asked to give a reason for the hope that is in us. Perhaps St. Francis of Assisi best summed up the message of James: "Preach the gospel at all times; use words if necessary."

"Lord, raise up more 'silent' witnesses to increase the harvest of souls entering your kingdom."

James 2:1-9

[1] My brothers and sisters, do you with your acts of favoritism really believe in our glorious Lord Jesus Christ? [2]For if a person with gold rings and in fine clothes comes into your assembly, and if a poor person in dirty clothes also comes in, [3]and if you take notice of the one wearing the fine clothes and say, "Have a seat here, please," while to the one who is poor you say, "Stand there," or, "Sit at my feet," [4]have you not made distinctions among yourselves, and become judges with evil thoughts? [5]Listen, my beloved brothers and sisters. Has not God chosen the poor in the world to be rich in faith and to be heirs of the kingdom that he has promised to those who love him? [6]But you have dishonored the poor. Is it not the rich who oppress you? Is it not they who drag you into court? [7]Is it not they who blaspheme the excellent name that was invoked over you?

[8] You do well if you really fulfill the royal law according to the scripture, "You shall love your neighbor as yourself." [9]But if you show partiality, you commit sin and are convicted by the law as transgressors.

You shall love your neighbor as yourself. (James 2:8)

We are called to love others as God has loved us—impartially. Every human being who ever existed has needed Jesus' atoning sacrifice on the cross, and Jesus made that sacrifice for everyone (Romans 3:23-24). He himself said that God loved us all so deeply that he gave his only Son so that *"everyone who believes in him may not perish but may have eternal life"* (John 3:16). Now, God calls us to have the same kind of love for one another (1 John 4:11).

Jesus died on the cross for *everyone*, and he longs to pour out the Holy Spirit into everyone's heart. He has made us all co-heirs with him, sons and daughters of his Father, equal members of his church, all with the same dignity. When we show favoritism or partiality toward our fellow human beings, we are really speaking against the cross of Christ, because partiality implies an unequal need for the cross—that some are more deserving of God's love than others are.

The great apostle Peter fell into this kind of thinking when Jesus told the disciples that he must suffer and die. Feeling, perhaps, that Jesus was too good to die, Peter rebuked him (Mark 8:32). It's as if he were saying, "No, Jesus, you don't deserve to die. Let someone else take your place." As Jesus' reply demonstrates, Peter was relying only on human thinking (8:33). Jesus was fully human, just like us, in all things but sin. And it was only through his death that he could begin to heal the divisions existing among people.

The universality of Jesus' death is implicit in the command "Love your neighbor as yourself" (James 2:8). When we show God's impartial love to those around us, we declare the truth about who God is: he is love (1 John 4:8). There is no contempt in God—no preference, no division. By the Spirit he gave us, we can love impartially. Jesus did it by dying for all of us, and through his death, it is possible for us, too.

"Jesus, you want us to be one as you and the Father are one.

Come, Lord, and break down all divisions. Pour out your love through the Holy Spirit, that we would love as you have loved us. Destroy the divisions that argue against your cross."

James 2:10-13

[10]For whoever keeps the whole law but fails in one point has become accountable for all of it. [11]For the one who said, "You shall not commit adultery," also said, "You shall not murder." Now if you do not commit adultery but if you murder, you have become a transgressor of the law. [12]So speak and so act as those who are to be judged by the law of liberty. [13]For judgment will be without mercy to anyone who has shown no mercy; mercy triumphs over judgment.

Mercy triumphs over judgment. (James 2:13)

At the conclusion of Dickens' immortal tale *A Christmas Carol*, Ebenezer Scrooge awakens from a terrible and frightening dream. Suddenly, this old curmudgeon, known mostly for his bad temper, starts laughing! He laughs so hard that the neighbors think that he has finally "gone around the bend." Only yesterday he was muttering, "Bah, humbug!" when people wished him a merry Christmas, and now he is buying a prize turkey for his clerk, making huge donations to charity, and visiting all the relatives he had ignored for years. What happened?

To explain Scrooge's transformation, we don't need to look any further than James. Scrooge is a perfect example of the person James is talking about here. He had pursued success and forgotten about other people. He didn't know how to show mercy—until he understood how much he needed it himself. Seeing a vision of his own death, he pleaded for compassion with the Spirit of Christmas Future. "I am not the man I was," he insisted.

When the vision disappeared and he found himself alive, Scrooge was ecstatic. He knew, somehow, that he had been forgiven—given a second chance; and he couldn't wait to make up for lost time by doing as much good as possible. One translation of James puts it this way: "Mercy can afford to laugh at judgment."

As Scrooge shows us, to "laugh at judgment" does not mean to laugh at God's justice but rather to rejoice at his mercy! When we have experienced the mercy of God as Scrooge did, we cannot help but be joyful. When we know Jesus' everlasting love, we will no longer live in fear, because "perfect love casts out fear" (1 John 4:18). We don't have to be just "do-gooders"; we can be *apostles* who bring Christ into every situation.

Can we, like Scrooge, learn how to keep Christmas all year long? Of course we can, and we should. How else will the kingdom of God get built? So go ahead and seek the Lord with your whole heart. Immerse yourself in prayer and Scripture. Seek the fellowship of committed Christians. Let the sacramental life of the church fill you with every grace and blessing. If we stay close to the Lord in these ways, we will not only have some*thing* to give to others—like food, or clothing, or a kind word—but some*one*! We'll have Jesus himself. He came to bring fire to the earth (Luke 12:49). So let's all go out and carry his light to the world!

"Lord, help me to live in your mercy. May I become so full of your love that I always have enough to share!"

James 2:14-26

14   What good is it, my brothers and sisters, if you say you have faith but do not have works? Can faith save you? 15If a brother or sister is naked and lacks daily food, 16and one of you says to them, "Go in peace; keep warm and eat your fill," and yet you do not supply their bodily needs, what is the good of that? 17So faith by itself, if it has no works, is dead.

18   But someone will say, "You have faith and I have works." Show me your faith apart from your works, and I by my works will show you my faith. 19You believe that God is one; you do well. Even the demons believe—and shudder. 20Do you want to be shown, you senseless person, that faith apart from works is barren? 21Was not our ancestor Abraham justified by works when he offered his son Isaac on the altar? 22You see that faith was active along with his works, and faith was brought to completion by the works. 23Thus the scripture was fulfilled that says, "Abraham believed God, and it was reckoned to him as righteousness," and he was called the friend of God. 24You see that a person is justified by works and not by faith alone. 25Likewise, was not Rahab the prostitute also justified by works when she welcomed the messengers and sent them out by another road? 26For just as the body without the spirit is dead, so faith without works is also dead.

For nearly five centuries, Roman Catholic and Lutheran Christians have been divided over the issue of justification by faith. In one sense, the struggle to understand justification goes back even further, as illustrated by the debate in James: "Show me your faith apart from your works, and I by my works will show you my faith. . . . You see that a person is justified by works and not by faith alone" (James 2:18, 24).

Recently, however, the Holy Spirit moved leaders from both churches to discuss their differences in the hopes of bringing about a deeper unity. For thirty years, representatives have been meeting, trying to discern the common ground between Lutherans and Catholics. As a result, the Vatican and the World Lutheran Federation issued a *Joint Declaration on the Doctrine of Justification* in October of 1999. In one of its most dramatic statements, the declaration states, "Together we confess: By grace alone, in faith in Christ's saving work and not because of any merit on our part, we are accepted by God and receive the Holy Spirit, who renews our hearts while equipping and calling us to good works" (15).

The document also points out that, in spite of differences in theological language and emphasis, the fundamental understanding of Catholics and Lutherans remains the same: "When Catholics say that persons 'cooperate' in . . . accepting justification, they see such personal consent as itself an effect of grace, not as an action arising from innate human abilities" (20). And both mutually confess that "good works—a Christian life lived in faith, hope and love—follow justification and are its fruits" (37). Together, they conclude that Lutheran and Catholic views on justification are "open to one another and do not destroy the consensus regarding basic truths" (40).

Let us join the declaration's authors in thanking God for this "decisive step forward on the way to overcoming the division of the church" (44). Let us pray that this movement of the Holy Spirit toward full unity will continue.

"Make us one, Lord, that the world may know we are your disciples by our love."

James 3:1-12

¹ Not many of you should become teachers, my brothers and sisters, for you know that we who teach will be judged with greater strictness. ²For all of us make many mistakes. Anyone who makes no mistakes in speaking is perfect, able to keep the whole body in check with a bridle. ³If we put bits into the mouths of horses to make them obey us, we guide their whole bodies. ⁴Or look at ships: though they are so large that it takes strong winds to drive them, yet they are guided by a very small rudder wherever the will of the pilot directs. ⁵So also the tongue is a small member, yet it boasts of great exploits.

How great a forest is set ablaze by a small fire! ⁶And the tongue is a fire. The tongue is placed among our members as a world of iniquity; it stains the whole body, sets on fire the cycle of nature, and is itself set on fire by hell. ⁷For every species of beast and bird, of reptile and sea creature, can be tamed and has been tamed by the human species, ⁸but no one can tame the tongue—a restless evil, full of deadly poison. ⁹With it we bless the Lord and Father, and with it we curse those who are made in the likeness of God. ¹⁰From the same mouth come blessing and cursing. My brothers and sisters, this ought not to be so. ¹¹Does a spring pour forth from the same opening both fresh and brackish water? ¹²Can a fig tree, my brothers and sisters, yield olives, or a grapevine figs? No more can salt water yield fresh.

The tongue is a small member, yet it boasts of great exploits. (James 3:5)

Stephen is a marvelous example of how the words we speak reveal the thoughts of our hearts. In response to accusations that he spoke blasphemies, Stephen boldly proclaimed the resurrection of Christ. Even as he was being stoned to death, he cried out,

"Lord, do not hold this sin against them" (Acts 7:60).

Stephen's words manifested a heart filled with divine love. He didn't condemn his killers. Instead, the love of God within him enabled him to overcome his suffering and bless those who cursed him. Like Stephen, we too can learn to dissolve our anger and hatred by turning to the Lord in times of need and suffering. The Lord will give us the grace to purify our thoughts, intentions, and desires so that, like Stephen, we can bless others—even when our human natures would have us do otherwise.

Jealous remarks, sarcastic words, arrogant or deceitful speech, or an inability to control a gossiping tongue are all indications that we are still bound to sin. They are markers that point out areas in our hearts that still need repentance and healing. By the same token, comforting, kind, and loving words—especially when we feel hurt or angry—demonstrate a trust and closeness to God.

Let us take a look at what comes out of our mouths. Learning to control our tongues is another way of taking control of our hearts and turning them over to Jesus. As we turn to God for help in expressing his love for others, we will learn to take our thoughts captive and overcome some of the pitfalls that seem regularly to trip us up. When we are hurt, anger naturally comes out of our mouths. Supernaturally, however, God can take our bitterness and transform it into purity of heart. Let us surrender our tongues to God as we experience deliverance from sin and bondage to our fallen nature.

"Jesus, purify my heart. Turn my anger and bitterness into love and kindness—even toward those who hurt me. Let the world see that my intentions flow from my love for you."

James 3:13-18

[13] Who is wise and understanding among you? Show by your good life that your works are done with gentleness born of wisdom. [14]But if you have bitter envy and selfish ambition in your hearts, do not be boastful and false to the truth. [15]Such wisdom does not come down from above, but is earthly, unspiritual, devilish. [16]For where there is envy and selfish ambition, there will also be disorder and wickedness of every kind. [17]But the wisdom from above is first pure, then peaceable, gentle, willing to yield, full of mercy and good fruits, without a trace of partiality or hypocrisy. [18]And a harvest of righteousness is sown in peace for those who make peace.

Who is wise and understanding among you? Show by your good life that your works are done with gentleness born of wisdom. (James 3:13)

Solanus Casey was a priest who fully exemplified the gentleness and wisdom James calls for in this passage. The son of a Wisconsin farmer, Casey failed out of his diocesan seminary but was undeterred in his quest to become a priest. He was able to gain entry into the Capuchin Franciscans, but because of his poor academics, his superiors stipulated that he could neither hear confessions nor preach homilies. Casey was so grateful to God for his priesthood that this unusual restriction didn't really bother him.

For forty years, Fr. Solanus worked as the doorkeeper of a Detroit friary. Because of his extraordinary gift of counsel, his holiness, and his many miracles of healing, he received thousands of visitors, many of whom were deeply touched by the Lord through him. His death in 1957 was mourned not only by his fellow Capuchins and the people of Detroit, but by believers throughout the country and even around the world. One woman wrote of him: "He never let us feel he was hurried, giving each person as much of his time as we desired. The meekness of his manner and his extremely low voice and sincere desire to help each of us are things I remember."

Casey's life teaches us some important lessons about meekness and humility. First, it is not as hard as we think! If we always acknowledge God's greatness and goodness, as Fr. Solanus did, we find it much easier to get rid of our self-will, or as one writer calls it, the "Disease of Me." Second, when we give everything to God, the rewards far outweigh the sacrifices. As Jesus told us, "Unless a grain of wheat falls into the earth and dies, it remains just a single grain; but if it dies, it bears much fruit" (John 12:24).

As Fr. Solanus' life also demonstrates, wisdom doesn't necessarily come from being the smartest in the class. In the weakness of our flesh, we don't even know how to love our neighbor as we should. But the Spirit will give us the heavenly wisdom James speaks of, a wisdom that will help us to understand God's laws with our hearts as well as with our heads. It's not complicated! Solanus Casey, who would be the first to call himself an ordinary person, would give us the same advice James does: "If any of you is lacking in wisdom, ask God, who gives to all generously and ungrudgingly, and it will be given you" (James 1:5).

"Lord, give me the gift of always being grateful to you, as Fr. Solanus was. Give me the desire to know you and seek you above any earthly thing, so that I may be truly wise."

James 4:1-10

[1] Those conflicts and disputes among you, where do they come from? Do they not come from your cravings that are at war within you? [2] You want something and do not have it; so you commit mur-

der. And you covet something and cannot obtain it; so you engage in disputes and conflicts. You do not have, because you do not ask. ³You ask and do not receive, because you ask wrongly, in order to spend what you get on your pleasures. ⁴Adulterers! Do you not know that friendship with the world is enmity with God? Therefore whoever wishes to be a friend of the world becomes an enemy of God. ⁵Or do you suppose that it is for nothing that the scripture says, "God yearns jealously for the spirit that he has made to dwell in us"? ⁶But he gives all the more grace; therefore it says,

"God opposes the proud,
    but gives grace to the humble."

⁷Submit yourselves therefore to God. Resist the devil, and he will flee from you. ⁸Draw near to God, and he will draw near to you. Cleanse your hands, you sinners, and purify your hearts, you double-minded. ⁹Lament and mourn and weep. Let your laughter be turned into mourning and your joy into dejection. ¹⁰Humble yourselves before the Lord, and he will exalt you. ☙

God created us to know and love him. He wants us to experience his grace ruling in our hearts. And so, as an experienced pastor, James used his letter to exhort his congregation to deepen their conversion to Christ to the point where faith and deeds go hand in hand. To see that accomplished, he pointed them toward the decisive battle being waged over the desires of their hearts. By teaching his people the way of victory in this battle, James knew that he could lead them to a deeper life in Jesus.

God doesn't want his people to be glum or battle-weary. Rather, he wants joyful and peaceful children who are happy to serve him. The kind of joy that God wants to give us comes as we allow him to search us and purify us of sin. Without this ongoing purification, our service of God may be of little value or effect. This is a sometimes painful discovery, but as James wrote, God gives us grace and jealously watches over us to bring us to a full life in him (James 4:5-6).

We need to draw near to God so that he will draw near to us (James 4:8). As we come into his presence, we will learn that the things of the world will not satisfy us. We belong to God and therefore have received divine power over our fallen passions and desires. He is a loving God who is serious about sin and its effects on his church.

True joy comes in learning that the desires and passions that are opposed to God have been fully dealt with by the cross of Christ. By drawing near to Jesus, we can be freed from sin. As imperfect servants striving to let God's grace rule our lives, we can come to the Lord and be delivered from the desires and passions that separate us from him. We can be strengthened to live in accord with what Jesus has taught us.

"Lord Jesus, we want to draw near to you. By the power of your cross, free us from desires and passions that separate us from you. We want to become more like you."

James 4:11-12

[11] Do not speak evil against one another, brothers and sisters. Whoever speaks evil against another or judges another, speaks evil against the law and judges the law; but if you judge the law, you are not a doer of the law but a judge. [12]There is one lawgiver and judge who is able to save and to destroy. So who, then, are you to judge your neighbor?

Do we have any idea of the power of words? We know from looking at history that words can build nations and bring down kingdoms. But have you ever stopped to think that it was a word from God that created the world? Or that Jesus Christ is the Word made flesh who was with God from the beginning? Considering the awesome power God has given to words, it's amazing that he allows us the free will to use them as we please—and it is a terrible thing when we use them wrongly.

We know that uncharitable words can ruin reputations and cause untold anguish. But did you know that we really don't have the "legal" authority to utter them in the first place? We might be the plaintiff who believes that he or she has been wronged and deserves the right to rebuke the defendant, but only the "judge" can pass sentence. And his name is Jesus! The only one who seems to get away with accusing everyone is Satan—and he has already been condemned! In truth, gossip and slander hurt us more than they hurt the people we are talking about. "On the day of judgment you will have to give an account for every careless word you utter; for by your words you will be justified, and by your words you will be condemned" (Matthew 12:36-37).

If you have said something that has caused harm to someone else, try to undo the damage by apologizing. But then try to go one step further. Look into your heart to try to discover why you said what you said. Is it possible that you have allowed anger or an unwillingness to forgive control you? Has envy gotten the upper hand? Or perhaps fear and mistrust? Don't hesitate to turn these issues over to the Lord! He wants to heal you, not condemn you.

In addition to avoiding critical speech, there is one more thing that we can do, and that is to make a habit of *helpful* speech. Our words can be a powerful source of strength and encouragement. When spoken in the love of Christ, they can even bring hope and healing to those who are hurting. Paul advises, "Let no evil talk come out of your mouths, but only what is useful for building up, as

THE CHURCH MOVES OUT

there is need, so that your words may give grace to those who hear" (Ephesians 4:29). So remember that "death and life are in the power of the tongue" (Proverbs 18:21). The choice is ours.

"Lord, I praise you for the gift of speech! Cleanse my heart of any bitterness, so that my words may never harm, but always help."

James 4:13-17

¹³ Come now, you who say, "Today or tomorrow we will go to such and such a town and spend a year there, doing business and making money." ¹⁴Yet you do not even know what tomorrow will bring. What is your life? For you are a mist that appears for a little while and then vanishes. ¹⁵Instead you ought to say, "If the Lord wishes, we will live and do this or that." ¹⁶As it is, you boast in your arrogance; all such boasting is evil. ¹⁷Anyone, then, who knows the right thing to do and fails to do it, commits sin.

Using an expression that goes back to the New Testament church, many Arab Christians end their conversations with, "if God wills." "I will see you next week, if God wills." Paul used this expression when he addressed the Christians at Corinth: "I will come to you soon, if the Lord wills" (1 Corinthians 4:19). Similarly, James reminds us that our future is in God's control. We can make the best of plans, but only God can guarantee the future.

If this is the case, wouldn't it make sense simply to sit on our front porches, awaiting the second coming? No. We must always be prepared to face the Lord, but still remain free from anxiety and preoccupation over the future (Matthew 6:25). To make this point,

37

Jesus used an illustration from nature. If God provides so abundantly for the birds and the flowers, how much more can we, his
very children, rely on his care? In the Lord's Prayer, we are reminded
that God is our provider when we pray, "Give us this day our daily
bread." Bread is the very staple of life, a symbol of all that we need
to live and grow.

Anxiety is neither helpful nor necessary to our lives. It robs us of
our faith in God's providence and saps our energy. Jesus admonishes
us to put away such anxiety and seek the things of God instead.
It's not hard to see how both anxiety and boastful self-reliance are
based on the false assumption that we can somehow control our
future.

How, then, should we live? Should we passively resign ourselves
to fate? No. But neither should we become so consumed by worry
that we lose our focus on the one who provides for all our needs.
God wants to place our hope in him and in the future he promised
us. Don't let the cares of this world make you afraid. And don't
let your worries convince you that you've got to overcome every
obstacle on your own. Instead, turn to God and surrender your
future into his hands. Ask his Spirit to help you let go of worry and
live in the light of his promises.

"Lord, free me from needless worry and preoccupation. I want to
abandon myself to your plan. May I live every day with trust and
gratitude for your providential care."

James 5:1-6

[1] Come now, you rich people, weep and wail for the miseries that
are coming to you. [2]Your riches have rotted, and your clothes are
moth-eaten. [3]Your gold and silver have rusted, and their rust will

be evidence against you, and it will eat your flesh like fire. You have laid up treasure for the last days. ⁴Listen! The wages of the laborers who mowed your fields, which you kept back by fraud, cry out, and the cries of the harvesters have reached the ears of the Lord of hosts. ⁵You have lived on the earth in luxury and in pleasure; you have fattened your hearts in a day of slaughter. ⁶You have condemned and murdered the righteous one, who does not resist you.

Oftentimes, even God's people find themselves living in pursuit of money and possessions while ignoring the needs of the poor. This happened to the people of Israel during the years just before the fall of the northern kingdom in 721 B.C. As Israel grew in prosperity, many of her wealthy began to disregard their duties to the poor. In seeking higher profits, they began trading with the nations around them and soon became enamored by the false gods that these pagans worshipped. As a result, they abandoned their covenant with Yahweh. In their case, abandonment of the poor led to abandonment of the Lord.

Jesus wants to rouse us from our tendency toward selfishness so that we will consider the purpose of our lives and the real treasure we should be accumulating. "I was hungry and you gave me food, I was thirsty and you gave me something to drink, I was a stranger and you welcomed me, I was naked and you gave me clothing, I was sick and you took care of me, I was in prison and you visited me" (Matthew 25:35-36). Only when we have done these things will Jesus say to us, "Come, you that are blessed by my Father, inherit the kingdom prepared for you from the foundation of the world" (25:34).

Caring for our brothers and sisters in need is our duty as followers of Jesus. It is not an option. In a world struggling with sin, poverty will always be a reality. To love the poor is a privilege that God gives to us—a constant antidote for natural selfishness and a way to make our faith visible. Jesus is indeed present among us today, but in what Mother Teresa often called "the distressing disguise of the poor."

We can find great joy in obeying the biblical command to love the poor among us. Look around! There is no lack of opportunity: needy families in our public schools, new immigrants struggling to find jobs, homeless men and women living in cardboard boxes, entire countries ground down by crippling poverty. Let us ask the Lord to lead us to his people and show us how we can learn to love him as we care for their needs.

"Lord, many of your children suffer poverty and injustice. Draw them to your heart. Help us become instruments of your peace."

James 5:7-12

7 Be patient, therefore, beloved, until the coming of the Lord. The farmer waits for the precious crop from the earth, being patient with it until it receives the early and the late rains. 8You also must be patient. Strengthen your hearts, for the coming of the Lord is near. 9Beloved, do not grumble against one another, so that you may not be judged. See, the Judge is standing at the doors! 10As an example of suffering and patience, beloved, take the prophets who spoke in the name of the Lord. 11Indeed we call blessed those who showed endurance. You have heard of the endurance of Job, and you have seen the purpose of the Lord, how the Lord is compassionate and merciful.

12 Above all, my beloved, do not swear, either by heaven or by earth or by any other oath, but let your "Yes" be yes and your "No" be no, so that you may not fall under condemnation. 〜

Beloved, do not grumble against one another. (James 5:9)

How often we fail to appreciate the power of our words! A negative comment or sarcastic remark can sour a relationship. Constant complaining and grumbling among family members can cast a shadow over a household that lasts for a very long time. Thankfully, the reverse is also true. A kind word or smile can lift someone's spirits, and encouragement or praise can give a friend the courage to take the next hard step on a difficult journey.

Much of what we say is a reflection of what is in our hearts. If we are feeling angry or resentful, it is much more likely that our words will be negative. If we are thinking critically about a person, we probably won't be very loving or encouraging toward him or her. The key to controlling our tongues lies in unburdening our hearts to the Lord in prayer and asking for his forgiveness for any sin or hard-heartedness we might have against someone else.

God can turn our stony hearts into hearts like his as we surrender to him. Even when it is necessary to correct someone, we can do it in a loving way, by pointing out the fault without condemning the person. Everyone needs correction from time to time. But often, the way someone responds to correction or criticism will depend on how it's delivered.

Words of kindness, encouragement, praise, and gratitude are the balm in any relationship—especially for husbands and wives. In Mark's gospel, Jesus reveals his Father's plan for married love: "From the beginning of creation, 'God made them male and female. For this reason a man shall leave his father and mother and be joined to his wife, and the two shall become one flesh.' So they are no longer two but one flesh" (Mark 10:6-8). This plan can become a reality when spouses make a point of encouraging and blessing each other with frequent expressions of love and kindness. Such gentle and loving communication can become the soil where the fruits of trust and unity can grow. The tongue has great power. Let us use it to strengthen our relationships, not tear them down. Let our words be a mirror of pure hearts on fire for God and for one another.

"Father, in the sacrament of marriage, you join a man and woman together as one. Pour out your grace on every marriage, especially those that are struggling. May every marriage give glory to you, the source of all love and unity."

James 5:13-20

13 Are any among you suffering? They should pray. Are any cheerful? They should sing songs of praise. 14Are any among you sick? They should call for the elders of the church and have them pray over them, anointing them with oil in the name of the Lord. 15The prayer of faith will save the sick, and the Lord will raise them up; and anyone who has committed sins will be forgiven. 16Therefore confess your sins to one another, and pray for one another, so that you may be healed. The prayer of the righteous is powerful and effective. 17Elijah was a human being like us, and he prayed fervently that it might not rain, and for three years and six months it did not rain on the earth. 18Then he prayed again, and the heaven gave rain and the earth yielded its harvest.

19 My brothers and sisters, if anyone among you wanders from the truth and is brought back by another, 20you should know that whoever brings back a sinner from wandering will save the sinner's soul from death and will cover a multitude of sins.

I t is unfortunate but true that we sometimes tell someone, "I'll pray for you," but never really do. That may be because we think of praying for a person as a last resort, or as a substitute for actually *doing* something that will help change his or her situation. But God wants us to know that prayer is the best thing we *can* do for someone! As Alfred Lord Tennyson once wrote, "More things are wrought by prayer than this world dreams of."

In giving us the example of Elijah, who was a human being just like us, James wants to show us that our prayers really do matter. If Elijah's prayers were used to shape the history of Israel, then there is no telling what God has in mind for us. Since the time of Jesus, the prayers of the saints have healed the sick, cast out demons, ended wars, and even raised the dead. Maybe we think those prayers only work for saints. But we tend to forget that the saints were human beings, just like Elijah and just like us! Why should we think that God could not choose to work through us, as well?

God is all-powerful. He doesn't need anyone's prayers. Still, he chooses to work through us anyway. That one simple fact should make us jump with excitement! Prayer is not only the way we commune with the Lord, it's also the way he fulfills his will in this world. Scripture tells us, for example, that God is looking for someone to "stand in the breach" and pray for his people (Ezekiel 22:30). And God tells Daniel, who is praying for Israel's return from exile, "Your words have been heard, and I have come because of your words" (Daniel 10:12).

As we reflect on the prayer of intercession, let's thank God for giving us such an important means of cooperating in his work. And let's look for the opportunities he gives us to intercede for others. When you feel a tug in your heart to pray for a friend, don't assume that it can wait, or that your friend will be all right regardless. That tug just may be God prompting you! Or if you see something wrong in your community, or even in your country, don't assume that the "super saints" will take care of it. Your prayers are vital to

LIVE OUT YOUR FAITH

God's plans—so don't miss out on your chance to bring about his kingdom's reign on earth!

"Lord, I ask for the desire to intercede. Let me understand the authority I have as your child to pray in faith for your people. In your name, let me move mountains!"

Baptized into a New Dignity

The First Letter of Peter

BAPTIZED INTO A NEW DIGNITY

Baptized into a New Dignity
An Introduction to the First Letter of Peter

Rev. Jude Winkler, OFM Conv

Once in a while when we are reading Scripture, we run across a gem that we didn't even know was there. This is the impression many people have when they read the First Letter of Peter. It is not all that long, only 105 verses, or even all that original—many of its ideas can be found in other writings of the New Testament. But it is unique for its incredibly positive attitude. It speaks of the tremendous dignity into which we are all called through our baptism. It explains that the sufferings we endure when we give witness to our beliefs are an honor, a participation in the passion of Christ. It even instructs us about how we can make our everyday actions a glowing witness to our faith.

Who Wrote 1 Peter? The author of this letter identifies himself as Peter the apostle. But did he really write it? It was not uncommon for first-century authors to write under a pseudonym, attributing their works to a famous personality. Scholars, in fact, have suggested that at least a few of the books of the New Testament may fall into that category—including 1 Peter.

What is the evidence? The author calls himself Peter (1 Peter 1:1). He describes himself as a leader of the Christian community and a witness of Christ's suffering and glory (5:1). He uses shepherd imagery, recalling Peter's mandate to be the chief shepherd of the church (John 21:15-19). All of this seems to point to Peter the apostle, so why would we doubt Peter's authorship?

One reason, some scholars say, is that the language and content don't sound as if they were produced by an uneducated fisherman from Galilee. For one thing, the Greek is much better than one would expect of a tradesman. Furthermore, much of the content of 1 Peter is found in the letters of Paul and James. So it's possible that this is just a compilation of other people's writings.

How can we answer the questions raised by these observations? One way is to look at the letter itself. At the end of the letter, we hear that Silvanus (also called Silas) was the actual writer, acting as Peter's secretary (1 Peter 5:12). In the ancient world, this could mean that Peter dictated the letter while Silvanus copied it down word for word, or it could mean that Peter gave the general ideas to Silvanus, who then elaborated the letter using his own words. So it is possible that Silvanus did much of the work of writing this letter. This would help explain the better Greek—since it was Silvanus' and not Peter's Greek—as well as the connection with Paul's ideas, since Silvanus was also a disciple of Paul.

Weighing these factors, as well as others, most scholars consider it fair to say that Peter could have written the letter through Silvanus, and that those who doubt Peter's authorship have the burden of proof.

When and Why. Peter tells us that he is writing from "Babylon." In the early church, the name of this ancient city was a code phrase for Rome. So Peter probably wrote his letter from Rome in the years shortly before his martyrdom (in the late sixties).

This letter is unusual in that it was not written to correct any problems in the community, as is the case with most of the other letters in the New Testament. Instead, this is a letter of encouragement and exhortation. Peter develops the theme that we Christians have been called to an incredible dignity, and we must now live in that dignity, through honorable lives of everyday witness to our faith.

Our Baptismal Dignity. The source of our dignity is our baptism. There is so much baptismal symbolism in this letter that some scholars have suggested that it might have originated as a baptismal instruction or possibly a homily at the Easter Vigil, when catechumens were received into the church.

Peter marvels over the fact that in baptism we have been born again to an imperishable life (1 Peter 1:3-4). He goes on to tell his readers that they are living stones in the temple of the church (2:5); a chosen race, a royal priesthood, a holy nation (2:9) who are called to be holy as God is holy (1:16).

Peter's amazement at all we have received in baptism reflects an old Jewish maxim that in front of every human being flies a host of archangels who proclaim, "Fall on your knees before the image of the living God!" Created in God's image and likeness, we carry the very breath of God in our hearts. This is a high honor indeed, one that calls us to live in accord with the dignity conferred upon us. Seen in this light, sin is saying to ourselves and others that we are not very honorable, and so we may as well act dishonorably. The call to conversion in this letter is not based upon fear of punishment or an appeal to a guilty conscience but on a call to become everything that God has created us to be.

Living as Exiles. This transformation to a life of baptismal dignity means that we Christians are different. We have abandoned the false values that once guided our lives. We are no longer slaves to our passions (1 Peter 4:3). We choose instead to live sober and prayerful lifestyles (4:2) dedicated to charity and hospitality (4:8-9). We live lives of quiet witness in obedience to those whom God has given authority over us (2:13, 18).

This is why Peter writes "to the exiles" of the provinces of northern Turkey (1 Peter 1:1). They are not exiles from a particular *place*. They are exiles from a former *way of life* (2:11). Our true home is heaven; our goal is salvation. We live in the world, but we are not of this world.

Even though he taught his readers that they are exiles, Peter did not expect them to separate themselves from society like an exclusive cult. Rather, he gives advice on how they should live out their Christian values in their everyday lives. We are to be obedient to those who govern us (1 Peter 2:13). Slaves are to be obedient to their masters (2:18). Wives are to be obedient to their husbands (3:1), and husbands are to honor their wives (3:7). Peter does not speak of the great things that people could do, for few of us ever accomplish truly great things. He advises Christians to do small things with faith. It is in the everyday things that we give our greatest witness. It is in our quiet, modest, sober lifestyles that we show how love can conquer evil.

The Cost of Discipleship. Living a life of quiet Christian heroism makes us different from those around us. They will notice that we have rejected our former ways, and they might resent us and even persecute us for what we have become (1 Peter 4:4). They may very well interpret our conduct as an implicit indictment against their own lives.

This is as true today as it was in the days of Peter. Being a Christian means making choices that set us apart, such as in the way we dress (1 Peter 3:3), the way we deal with suffering (4:13), the way we live chastely (2:11), and the love we bear for one another (1:22). We have to make choices concerning what we will watch on television, what type of vacation we will take, how we will interpret "having a good time," etc.

Peter is clear that making choices like these may well bring rejection and suffering. It's important to note that this letter was written before Christians were being persecuted in any widespread manner. When Peter talked about suffering, he was probably not speaking of the "red martyrdom" of being arrested, put on trial, and executed. He was speaking about "white martyrdom," the suffering that comes from being misunderstood, alienated, frustrated. It is what St. Thérèse of Lisieux once called the martyrdom of pinpricks.

The Gift of Suffering. Peter's approach to this kind of suffering is probably the most countercultural message found in this letter. Rather than seeing suffering as a sign of God's punishment or a curse, Peter speaks about it as being a participation in the sufferings of Christ (1 Peter 4:13), as a way of following in his footprints (2:21). For Peter, it is better to suffer for doing right than for doing wrong (2:20). Suffering teaches us patience and hope, since we live in light of eternity and not what is transitory (1:24-25). Suffering can even fill us with joy (4:13) when we come to see that something very holy is going on. Suffering purifies our faith (1:7) for it helps us to sort out the selfish motivations that might be behind our actions (our own interests as opposed to true charity).

Today suffering is often seen as something wrong. People ask, "What did I do to deserve this?" as if it were a punishment for a particular sin. Peter asked the same question, but in a different way: "What did I do to deserve this? Why would God treat me with so much dignity that he would invite me into this honor?" And what is that honor? Precisely the opportunity to witness to the power of Jesus' resurrection over death in all of its manifestations.

Preaching to the Spirits in Prison. While this letter was not written to correct any doctrinal mistake, it does contain one significant teaching. What did Jesus do after he died on the cross? In 3:19 we hear that he spoke to the "spirits in prison." We sometimes hear this referred to as his descent into "Hades," or the "Underworld" or "Sheol" or even "Hell." Peter was not speaking about the place of eternal punishment. Rather, he was speaking of the belief that when Jesus died, he descended into the underworld to invite those holy people into heaven who have lived good lives but who did not know him.

Interestingly, although this belief is only found here and in Ephesians 4:7-10, it was one of the earliest themes depicted in early Christian art. It is called the "Harrowing (or harvesting) of Hell." It was a way of explaining how people who had not been baptized could nevertheless be saved through Christ.

Difficulties. There are a couple of passages in 1 Peter that present a bit of difficulty for a modern reader. In 2:18, for example, Peter counsels slaves to be obedient to their masters. He never comes out and condemns the institution of slavery. There are two possible responses to this difficulty. First of all, Peter might not even be speaking of slavery as such. He actually uses a word that would more appropriately be translated as "belonging to one's household." This would include both slaves and domestic servants. Secondly, even if Peter did mean "slaves," he lived in a world in which slavery was an accepted reality. He is telling those who found themselves in this unfortunate state that it does not keep them from being good Christians. This is a good reminder to us today. Our faith is expressed not so much in what we do as in how we do it.

The other major difficulty is the way Peter speaks about women. He calls them the "weaker sex" (1 Peter 3:7) and tells wives to be submissive to their husbands (3:1). It must be remembered, however, that Peter was simply speaking about what was considered to be the proper order of things in his day. He did not challenge the status quo on a social level; instead, he gave his readers guidance on how they should respond to it spiritually. Furthermore, if husbands truly honor their wives as Peter tells them to do, what would it mean in today's world? Today we might use words like "respect" and "collaboration."

A Quiet Witness. Peter does not expect Christians to change the world through social or political revolution. He expects them to transform it into the image of the coming world through a life of quiet witness to virtue and obedience. Obedience does not mean subservience; it means living the life that God has called us to live, a life of dignity and ultimately of the glory that Peter himself witnessed. Peter is telling Christians that their small, everyday activities and thoughts and sacrifices are infinitely more powerful than one might ever think, for they are capable of manifesting the cross and resurrection of Christ.

BAPTIZED INTO A NEW DIGNITY

1 Peter 1:1-9

¹ Peter, an apostle of Jesus Christ,
To the exiles of the Dispersion in Pontus, Galatia, Cappadocia, Asia, and Bithynia, ²who have been chosen and destined by God the Father and sanctified by the Spirit to be obedient to Jesus Christ and to be sprinkled with his blood:
May grace and peace be yours in abundance.
³ Blessed be the God and Father of our Lord Jesus Christ! By his great mercy he has given us a new birth into a living hope through the resurrection of Jesus Christ from the dead, ⁴and into an inheritance that is imperishable, undefiled, and unfading, kept in heaven for you, ⁵who are being protected by the power of God through faith for a salvation ready to be revealed in the last time. ⁶In this you rejoice, even if now for a little while you have had to suffer various trials, ⁷so that the genuineness of your faith—being more precious than gold that, though perishable, is tested by fire—may be found to result in praise and glory and honor when Jesus Christ is revealed. ⁸Although you have not seen him, you love him; and even though you do not see him now, you believe in him and rejoice with an indescribable and glorious joy, ⁹for you are receiving the outcome of your faith, the salvation of your souls. 🕊

*Rejoice, even if now for a little while you have had to suffer
various trials. (1 Peter 1:6)*

Marie Léon Ramot, a twentieth-century French theologian, once wrote, "Bruised by suffering but carried on by their faith, prophets and wise men gradually enter into the mystery" of God and the wisdom of his plan. It's as if these "prophets and wise men" discover that God can bring good even out of the worst situations. Whatever the source or cause of pain and trial, for those who love God, suffering is always purifying and redemptive.

The apostles once asked Jesus why a certain man was born blind: "Who sinned, this man or his parents?" (John 9:2)? Jesus replied that it was not because of sin, but that the glory of God might be revealed. And with that, Jesus healed him. We do not know much about this man, but we do know that he was humble enough to recognize Jesus as the Messiah. The Pharisees and even the blind man's parents couldn't recognize Jesus, but this poor blind beggar was able to see the glory of God. Where once he had shared in Jesus' suffering, the blind man was now sharing in Jesus' glory (Romans 8:15-18).

God may not always remove our suffering the moment we ask him to. Still, he always seeks to console and comfort us in the midst of it. In fact, Scripture encourages us to endure suffering as a discipline that, though unpleasant, will in the end yield "the peaceful fruit of righteousness to those who have been trained by it" (Hebrews 12:7-11).

It is said that the saints love suffering but hate to suffer. They love suffering because of the blessings that accompany it. At the same time, they acknowledge how difficult it is to bear burdens and trials. Even Jesus prayed, "Remove this cup from me" (Mark 14:36). If God's Son struggled, how much more does God understand our desire not to face pain? Let us turn to God with our fears of suffering and let him reassure us of the good end he intends to make of all we endure.

"Lord, I pray for all those who cannot see your hand in their lives. Open their eyes to see that everything comes from you. Open their hearts to your comfort and consolation so that they may receive all the good you have for them."

1 Peter 1:10-16

¹⁰ Concerning this salvation, the prophets who prophesied of the grace that was to be yours made careful search and inquiry, ¹¹inquiring about the person or time that the Spirit of Christ within them indicated when it testified in advance to the sufferings destined for Christ and the subsequent glory. ¹²It was revealed to them that they were serving not themselves but you, in regard to the things that have now been announced to you through those who brought you good news by the Holy Spirit sent from heaven—things into which angels long to look!

¹³ Therefore prepare your minds for action; discipline yourselves; set all your hope on the grace that Jesus Christ will bring you when he is revealed. ¹⁴Like obedient children, do not be conformed to the desires that you formerly had in ignorance. ¹⁵Instead, as he who called you is holy, be holy yourselves in all your conduct; ¹⁶ for it is written, "You shall be holy, for I am holy."

How privileged we are to live in a time when Jesus has already won our salvation! Many prophets and righteous people have longed to see what we have seen and hear the word of salvation we have heard (Matthew 13:17). The good news from heaven has been made known to us—things that the angels longed to look upon (1 Peter 1:12). This letter calls all Christians to hope in Christ and to grow in holiness by being obedient children of the Father.

To be holy is to be set apart for God, to be consecrated to God, to live in right relationship with God. It is to be godlike. Only the new Adam, Jesus Christ, has attained the fullness of this purity and perfection of goodness and righteousness. As Christians, we are called to follow in Jesus' footsteps and be transformed into his likeness. We have the promise of Christ that he will always be with us through the indwelling Holy Spirit.

The Holy Spirit can lead us in the way of righteousness and holiness to which God calls us. As we open our minds to be taught by him in daily prayer, Scripture reading, and the teaching of the church, we will be transformed. Jesus gives us the chance to free our minds from the desires we hold in ignorance (1 Peter 1:14), through the power of the cross and the shedding of his blood. Every day we can lay claim to the gift of salvation given to us in baptism.

As we pray and seek to know the ways of God, the Holy Spirit will begin to fill our minds with the truth of God, rather than the principles of self. "Prepare your minds for action" (1 Peter 1:13). Expect that there will be a battle. Old memories of sin—perhaps resentments, angers, addictions—will try to dominate our thoughts, rather than the love and way of God. Remember that Jesus has overcome all sin by the shedding of his blood. All we need to do is make a conscious effort to give our lives to him.

"Heavenly Father, we put our hope and trust in you and in your Son, Jesus Christ. We ask that we may be made holy, as you are holy, so that we may become servants of the gospel, set apart to serve you and your church."

1 Peter 1:17-25

[17] If you invoke as Father the one who judges all people impartially according to their deeds, live in reverent fear during the time of your exile. [18]You know that you were ransomed from the futile ways inherited from your ancestors, not with perishable things like silver or gold, [19]but with the precious blood of Christ, like that of a lamb without defect or blemish. [20]He was destined before the foundation

THE CHURCH MOVES OUT

of the world, but was revealed at the end of the ages for your sake. [21]Through him you have come to trust in God, who raised him from the dead and gave him glory, so that your faith and hope are set on God.

[22] Now that you have purified your souls by your obedience to the truth so that you have genuine mutual love, love one another deeply from the heart. [23]You have been born anew, not of perishable but of imperishable seed, through the living and enduring word of God. [24]For

> "All flesh is like grass
>   and all its glory like the flower of grass.
> The grass withers,
>   and the flower falls,
> [25] but the word of the Lord endures forever."

That word is the good news that was announced to you.

Look at Peter's description of the riches we have gained in Christ—better than silver and gold, imperishable, precious (1 Peter 1:18-19)! The greatness of God's gift to us is unfathomable, and he sacrificed his own Son so that we could attain it. Now, as Peter pointed out, through "obedience to the truth" (1:22), our hearts are purified and we become a new creation in Christ. By turning from sin and accepting all that Jesus has done for us, we open the door for the Holy Spirit to empower us to obey the greatest of commands—the command to love one another.

Try to imagine the immensity of what we have received in Christ. Once slow to forgive and lacking in compassion, we now have the source of strength to love the unlovable, to forgive the unforgivable, and to obey every command God has ever given us. We now have the resources to live in complete submission to God's laws and ways.

59

What is your view of Christianity? Is it a matter of doing all the right things so that you can get into heaven? Or does it have at its core the calling and the promise that we can become like Jesus, who loved "to the point of death" (Philippians 2:8)? As impossible as this calling may seem to us, it is this very death of Christ that empowers us to live in love and obedience. Of ourselves, we are weak, yet through the cross, we are not only freed from sin but also granted a whole new life with the potential for Christlike obedience and humility.

How, then, can we grow in obedience? First, we must acknowledge that such a task is achieved "not by might, nor by power, but by [the] Spirit" (Zechariah 4:6). Second, we must set our wills never to say no to Jesus. At all times, we must seek to be attentive to his Spirit and be prepared to do what he asks of us. Through Christ, the way is opened. Sin is removed. Condemnation is lifted. We are recreated. What could possibly stand in the way of those whose hearts are set on the path of love and obedience that Jesus walked?

"Jesus, I thank you for making me a new creation through the shedding of your blood. Help me to see that obedience to your will is my soul's delight."

1 Peter 2:1-12

¹ Rid yourselves, therefore, of all malice, and all guile, insincerity, envy, and all slander. ²Like newborn infants, long for the pure, spiritual milk, so that by it you may grow into salvation—³if indeed you have tasted that the Lord is good.

⁴ Come to him, a living stone, though rejected by mortals yet chosen and precious in God's sight, and ⁵like living stones, let yourselves be built into a spiritual house, to be a holy priesthood, to offer

spiritual sacrifices acceptable to God through Jesus Christ. [6]For it stands in scripture:

"See, I am laying in Zion a stone,
a cornerstone chosen and precious;
and whoever believes in him
will not be put to shame."

[7]To you then who believe, he is precious; but for those who do not believe,

"The stone that the builders rejected
has become the very head of the corner,"

[8]and

"A stone that makes them stumble,
and a rock that makes them fall."

They stumble because they disobey the word, as they were destined to do.

[9] But you are a chosen race, a royal priesthood, a holy nation, God's own people, in order that you may proclaim the mighty acts of him who called you out of darkness into his marvelous light.

[10] Once you were not a people,
but now you are God's people;
once you had not received mercy,
but now you have received mercy.

[11] Beloved, I urge you as aliens and exiles to abstain from the desires of the flesh that wage war against the soul. [12]Conduct yourselves honorably among the Gentiles, so that, though they malign you as evildoers, they may see your honorable deeds and glorify God when he comes to judge. ✍

The First Letter of Peter was written sometime around 67 A.D., during the reign of the Roman emperor Nero. It was a time when many lived in extreme poverty while others held extravagant banquets. It was a time of sexual promiscuity and general disregard for human life. It was a time when Christians were in great need of encouragement and support. This is why St. Peter encouraged the believers in Asia Minor to stand firm in their convictions even when injustice, persecution, and worldly philosophies sought to rob them of their faith.

In many ways, our world today is not unlike those early days of the church. How often are we also tempted to give up as our faith is attacked, our dignity as children of God is eroded, and our hope in Christ is threatened?

Regardless of our age or circumstance, our heavenly Father wants us to trust that his plan has never changed. In his heart, we have always been "a chosen race, a royal priesthood, a holy nation, God's own people." At all times and in all places, Christians are called to "proclaim the mighty acts of him who called [us] out of darkness into his marvelous light" (1 Peter 2:9). This is the honor that is ours in Christ. God himself has chosen to work through us, not independently of us. As we surrender our hearts to him, his divine image is restored in us, and his indwelling Spirit enables us to bring Christ into the world.

Do you believe that Jesus can fill a room with his anointing and grace, just through your prayerful presence there? Do you believe that he can turn back the works of the devil in every situation where you are present? All this is possible, simply by the strength of our surrendered hearts. Let us walk confidently in the honor and authority we have been given. Let us pray today for opportunities to surrender our hearts that we might make Jesus present as we help a neighbor, intercede for an old friend, open a door for an elderly person, or listen attentively to a co-worker's concerns. As we do, Jesus' presence will lift their spirits and bring joy into our hearts.

"Light of Christ, come penetrate this darkness. May our surrendered hearts shine brightly for you in every place where the soles of our feet tread."

1 Peter 2:13-25

[13] For the Lord's sake accept the authority of every human institution, whether of the emperor as supreme, [14]or of governors, as sent by him to punish those who do wrong and to praise those who do right. [15]For it is God's will that by doing right you should silence the ignorance of the foolish. [16]As servants of God, live as free people, yet do not use your freedom as a pretext for evil. [17]Honor everyone. Love the family of believers. Fear God. Honor the emperor.

[18] Slaves, accept the authority of your masters with all deference, not only those who are kind and gentle but also those who are harsh. [19]For it is a credit to you if, being aware of God, you endure pain while suffering unjustly. [20]If you endure when you are beaten for doing wrong, what credit is that? But if you endure when you do right and suffer for it, you have God's approval. [21]For to this you have been called, because Christ also suffered for you, leaving you an example, so that you should follow in his steps.

[22] "He committed no sin,
  and no deceit was found in his mouth."

[23]When he was abused, he did not return abuse; when he suffered, he did not threaten; but he entrusted himself to the one who judges justly. [24]He himself bore our sins in his body on the cross, so that, free from sins, we might live for righteousness; by his wounds you have been healed. [25]For you were going astray like sheep, but now you have returned to the shepherd and guardian of your souls.

*As servants of God, live as free people, yet do not use your freedom
as a pretext for evil. (1 Peter 2:16)*

Those of us who lived through the 1960s and '70s witnessed
many misuses of freedom. Sloughing off social conventions
and moral restraints, "liberated" people not only inflicted
great pain on others but often wound up in bondage themselves,
whether to drugs, peer pressure, or just plain shallow thinking. The
truth is that no healthy human being can be completely unattached
or free from limitations. In many ways, we discover our personal
identity by making commitments. The important questions are *what*
we are going to commit ourselves to—and with what result. What
commitment is worth the investment of our whole lives?

Peter, of course, was one of the first to anchor his life to Jesus.
He found in this person everything he was seeking. Of course, his
relationship with Jesus didn't preserve him from doubt, confusion,
or even overwhelming demands, but it did give meaning to all those
experiences.

In this letter, Peter was addressing people limited by difficult
circumstances. All were citizens of an oppressive empire jealous
of other loyalties. Some were married to overbearing spouses who
didn't respect their Christian commitment. Others were slaves
whose masters were far from the "kind and gentle" spirit Peter called
for (1 Peter 2:18). Peter reminds all of these people of their union
with Christ—who himself was executed by the Roman Empire.
Precisely because Jesus did not resist his oppressors, he won true
freedom for his people, freedom from their ultimate enemy, death,
and its subversive henchman, sin.

What circumstances constrain us and appear to limit our freedom? Our own failing health? The burden of caring for dependent
parents or children? A dead-end job? What would "the glorious
liberty of the children of God" look like in these circumstances
(Romans 8:21)? In these circumstances, how might the Holy Spirit

be leading us to remain ever "mindful of God" and to live "as servants of God" (1 Peter 2:16)?

It may lead those who are facing life-threatening illness to a radical new diet and lifestyle. It may lead others to forego unnecessary procedures, refusing to let their lives revolve around their medical condition. It may lead some caregivers to humble themselves and ask the Christian community for help. It may lead others to see Christ in that dependent person and to free their spirits through unconditional love. It may lead some employees to do even more than the boss demands, and others to insist courageously on a different way of doing business.

The answers lie not so much in the specifics of what we should do as in how we should do it. For in all things, the key issue is honoring Jesus with our lives. This is how we can experience true freedom—even as we live our lives as humble servants of a loving Master.

"Lord, I offer you all my liberty. Show me how to put all my gifts at your disposal, expecting practical direction from your Holy Spirit."

1 Peter 3:1-7

¹ Wives, in the same way, accept the authority of your husbands, so that, even if some of them do not obey the word, they may be won over without a word by their wives' conduct, ²when they see the purity and reverence of your lives. ³Do not adorn yourselves outwardly by braiding your hair, and by wearing gold ornaments or fine clothing; ⁴rather, let your adornment be the inner self with the lasting beauty of a gentle and quiet spirit, which is very precious in God's sight. ⁵It was in this way long ago that the holy women who

hoped in God used to adorn themselves by accepting the authority of their husbands. ⁶Thus Sarah obeyed Abraham and called him lord. You have become her daughters as long as you do what is good and never let fears alarm you.

⁷   Husbands, in the same way, show consideration for your wives in your life together, paying honor to the woman as the weaker sex, since they too are also heirs of the gracious gift of life—so that nothing may hinder your prayers. ✍

D o you sometimes feel as if there is a blockage in your relationship with the Lord? While spiritual writers have devoted tomes to addressing these problems, Peter suggests we begin by taking a hard look at our human relationships. His advice is practical as well as radical: "Do what is good and never let fears alarm you" (1 Peter 3:6).

Like Paul, Peter tailored his advice to the individual circumstances of men and women. Women were under the authority of their husbands and would achieve little by opposing them directly. So instead, Peter advised them to win their husbands over by the example of their lives—not by outward adornments, but by the beauty of their inner character. And so that men would not abuse their earthly authority, Peter reminded them to honor and respect their wives as equal heirs with them of life in Christ—"so that nothing may hinder [their] prayers" (1 Peter 3:7).

Coupled with his advice to do the right thing is Peter's caution that we not be alarmed by our fears. Fears can impede our ability to do what we otherwise know is right and interfere with our relationships with one another and with the Lord.

For some of us, it may be fear of intimacy, which can prevent us from expressing our true feelings for one another for fear of getting hurt. Yet love necessarily involves risks, and without taking those risks, we miss out on all the benefits of a loving relationship.

For others, the fear of making mistakes or of disappointing others may hinder good relationships. As human beings, we are all going to make mistakes. What is important is that we learn to forgive one another—and also ourselves. No one made a bigger mistake than Peter made in denying Christ. He wept bitterly about it, but he accepted the Lord's forgiveness and learned to move forward totally dependent on grace.

Whatever our fears, we all need to accept that our true identity and our true healing lies with the living, interdependent body of Christ. Jesus doesn't necessarily promise to shield us from life's vicissitudes. Rather, he promises us something far greater: "I am with you always, to the end of the age" (Matthew 28:20).

"Lord, I long to be one with you and to please you in all I do. Reveal to me the hidden fears that hinder my relationship with you and with others. I surrender to you and believe that you can dissolve all my fears."

1 Peter 3:8-17

8 Finally, all of you, have unity of spirit, sympathy, love for one another, a tender heart, and a humble mind. 9Do not repay evil for evil or abuse for abuse; but, on the contrary, repay with a blessing. It is for this that you were called—that you might inherit a blessing. 10For

"Those who desire life
    and desire to see good days,
let them keep their tongues from evil
    and their lips from speaking deceit;
11 let them turn away from evil and do good;

> let them seek peace and pursue it.
>
> 12 For the eyes of the Lord are on the righteous,
>   and his ears are open to their prayer.
>   But the face of the Lord is against those who do evil."

13 Now who will harm you if you are eager to do what is good? 14But even if you do suffer for doing what is right, you are blessed. Do not fear what they fear, and do not be intimidated, 15but in your hearts sanctify Christ as Lord. Always be ready to make your defense to anyone who demands from you an accounting for the hope that is in you; 16yet do it with gentleness and reverence. Keep your conscience clear, so that, when you are maligned, those who abuse you for your good conduct in Christ may be put to shame. 17For it is better to suffer for doing good, if suffering should be God's will, than to suffer for doing evil. ✍

Do not repay evil for evil or abuse for abuse; but, on the contrary, repay with a blessing. It is for this that you were called—that you might inherit a blessing. (1 Peter 3:9)

Peter reminds us here that we are caught up in a grand circle of blessing. God stretches out his loving hand to bless us, and we pass along the blessing to the people around us. Then they "pay it forward" to others, and God rewards our generosity by blessing us. And so the gracious cycle continues.

Each of us is called both to give blessings and to be a blessing to the people around us. We automatically say "God bless you" when someone sneezes. Many parents bless their children at bedtime or whenever they leave the house, making the sign of the cross and invoking God's presence and protection. Laying hands on a friend who is ill or in need of comfort and invoking God's blessing on them is a very natural compassionate gesture.

That's how we *give* blessings. But how can we also *be* blessings? Peter describes people who are blessings to others as having "unity of spirit, sympathy, love for one another, a tender heart, and a humble mind" (1 Peter 3:8). He gives us another hint in verse 15: "Always be ready to make your defense to anyone who demands from you an account of the hope that is in you." Christians should be so optimistic and joy filled that their very demeanor makes people wonder why they are so peaceful. They need not go around proclaiming allegiance to the Lord; it will be so obvious as to invite queries.

Blessing those we care for—or even meet casually—is one thing, but Peter reminds us that we have a higher, more challenging vocation. Instead of returning reviling for reviling, we are to bless those who insult, malign, and persecute us. Jesus says, "Bless those who curse you, pray for those who abuse you" (Luke 6:28). Stephen's dying words echo Jesus' (Acts 7:60), and Paul gives the same advice: "Bless those who persecute you. . . . Do not repay anyone evil for evil. . . . Never avenge yourselves. . . . Do not be overcome by evil, but overcome evil with good" (Romans 12:14, 17, 19, 21).

How is this possible? By living in the power of the Holy Spirit. John reminds us, "The one who is in you is greater than the one who is in the world" (1 John 4:4). And so, the one who continues to bless us empowers us to bless others—especially those we may find most difficult to bless.

"Blessed are you, O Lord of mercy and compassion. You have overwhelmed me with blessings. Empower me to be a blessing to others, especially those most in need of your mercy."

1 Peter 3:18-22

[18]For Christ also suffered for sins once for all, the righteous for the unrighteous, in order to bring you to God. He was put to death in the flesh, but made alive in the spirit, [19]in which also he went and made a proclamation to the spirits in prison, [20]who in former times did not obey, when God waited patiently in the days of Noah, during the building of the ark, in which a few, that is, eight persons, were saved through water. [21]And baptism, which this prefigured, now saves you—not as a removal of dirt from the body, but as an appeal to God for a good conscience, through the resurrection of Jesus Christ, [22]who has gone into heaven and is at the right hand of God, with angels, authorities, and powers made subject to him.

This passage is a powerful meditation on baptism. Some commentators believe that Peter is quoting an early baptismal creed or hymn about Jesus, the one who was "put to death in the flesh, but made alive in the spirit, . . . has gone into heaven and is at the right hand of God, with angels, authorities, and powers made subject to him" (1 Peter 3:18, 21-22).

We tend to think of the story of Noah as a time in which God destroyed the world with water, but Peter saw it from a different perspective. Calling the event a precursor to baptism, he reminds us that it was through water that Noah and his family were saved.

Similarly, Peter invites us to see the water of baptism not just as an external cleansing or a new white garment. As in the time of Noah, baptism also saves us. It washes away our sinful past and gives us the opportunity for a radical new beginning, "an appeal to God for a good conscience, through the resurrection of Jesus Christ" (1 Peter 3:21). It confers upon us nothing less than Jesus' resurrected life and his own victory over sin and death.

As baptized believers, let's dare to plunge into the flood and abandon ourselves to God's transforming mercy. That flood may strip away old habits that have become second nature. It may separate us from relationships that are dragging us down. It may transport us to unfamiliar shores of service, to evangelize those we formerly saw as beyond God's sphere of influence. But in all of these situations, that flood is filled with God's refreshment, his vitality, and his overwhelming love.

Let's renew the commitment we made at our baptism so that we can rediscover our identity as beloved children who have been empowered to live as Jesus in the world today.

"Lord Jesus, I praise you for dying for my sins once for all so you might bring me to God. You have given me new birth by water and the Holy Spirit. Keep me faithful to you for ever and ever."

1 Peter 4:1-6

¹ Since therefore Christ suffered in the flesh, arm yourselves also with the same intention (for whoever has suffered in the flesh has finished with sin), ²so as to live for the rest of your earthly life no longer by human desires but by the will of God. ³You have already spent enough time in doing what the Gentiles like to do, living in licentiousness, passions, drunkenness, revels, carousing, and lawless idolatry. ⁴They are surprised that you no longer join them in the same excesses of dissipation, and so they blaspheme. ⁵But they will have to give an accounting to him who stands ready to judge the living and the dead. ⁶For this is the reason the gospel was proclaimed even to the dead, so that, though they had been judged in the flesh as everyone is judged, they might live in the spirit as God does.

B e prepared!" We're all familiar with the Boy Scout motto. Peter puts it this way: "Arm yourselves" (1 Peter 4:1). A police officer would be foolish to step between armed rival gangs without a bulletproof vest. It's prudent for boaters to don personal flotation devices. No one would jump out of an airplane without a parachute, or embark on a wilderness hike without food or water.

The kind of armor Peter is talking about is not a matter of physical protection or provision. "Arm yourselves . . . with the same intention" as Christ, he says. Be mentally prepared for what you are likely to encounter. There's nothing worse than being taken by surprise.

And what should we expect as we arm ourselves against assaults of temptation? To suffer—and to enjoy "the freedom of the glory of the children of God" (Romans 8:21). To be interrupted—and to discover God's invitation in the present moment. To endure hardship—and to experience the nearness of the one whose yoke we share (Matthew 11:28-30).

An experienced parent once told a new preschool teacher, "Expect to correct." Part of her job was to teach her students how to behave appropriately. If she expected them already to know how to behave, she was likely to react irritably when they didn't. If opportunities for gentle correction were built into her expectations, she could handle her real-life classroom with joyful equanimity.

Too often we barrel along with our own program and our own priorities. When something unexpected interrupts us, we are tempted to respond with ungraceful irritation. However, such interruptions can throw light in two directions, illuminating our own selfishness and pointing the way to God's will. Which is more important, finishing a chapter in a novel or praying with an upset friend who has mustered the courage to call and pour out her heart?

One way of arming ourselves to recognize God's call is to pause at the beginning of each day and seek direction. What situations do I know I will face today, and how can I bring Christ's love into them? As I wait in silence, is the Spirit enlivening a phrase from Scripture or a hymn that he would have me carry with me today, to use when and as he directs?

There's a battle going on out there. What kind of armor will you wear?

"Holy Spirit, help me put on your mind and arm myself with the firm intention of doing your will. Above all, clothe me in your love so that you are free to surprise me with your joyful summons."

1 Peter 4:7-11

7 The end of all things is near; therefore be serious and discipline yourselves for the sake of your prayers. 8Above all, maintain constant love for one another, for love covers a multitude of sins. 9Be hospitable to one another without complaining. 10Like good stewards of the manifold grace of God, serve one another with whatever gift each of you has received. 11Whoever speaks must do so as one speaking the very words of God; whoever serves must do so with the strength that God supplies, so that God may be glorified in all things through Jesus Christ. To him belong the glory and the power forever and ever. Amen. 🕉

The opening words of this passage seem to tell us that Peter has something important to say. "The end of all things is near," he warns. "Therefore be serious and discipline yourselves for the sake of your prayers. Above all . . . " (1 Peter 4:7-8). After such a dramatic, almost ominous buildup, we may disappointed at what comes next: "Maintain constant love for one another" (4:8). Doesn't it seem anticlimactic? We're on the verge of the apocalypse, and all Peter has to say is the "same old thing" about loving one another? But let's linger for a few moments with these simple words to let their full force sink in.

Why does Peter consider mutual love so important? Because he understood from personal experience that love has the power to cover "a multitude of sins" (1 Peter 4:8). Remember how, after Peter had denied even knowing him, Jesus sought Peter out and gave him a very intimate experience of his mercy (John 21:15-19)? Far from condemning him or expecting Peter to undo everything he had done, Jesus gave Peter a fresh opportunity to declare his love and allegiance and to start over again.

As Jesus treated Peter, so we too are called to treat one another. To "maintain constant love" in this way is necessarily to love unconditionally—without regard for whether another person lives according to our values or loves us in return. After all, Jesus loved us and gave his life for us "while we were still sinners" (Romans 5:8).

Maintaining constant love also means that we need to look beyond others' hurtful actions or words to discover their underlying cause, for the sake of preserving our relationships. If, for instance, I can get beyond the hurt I feel because of my sister's cross words to me this morning, then perhaps I can wonder whether there is something in her life that is causing her stress. And then, perhaps, I'll be able to do something to help. We've all heard of family members who have stopped speaking to one another for months—or even years—at a time. How sad, when they may not even remember the action or comment that created the hurt feelings in the first place! Peter's letter reminds us that life is too short to let anything get in the way of love.

If we answer the call to love one another, then the rest of Peter's advice follows naturally from it. We should practice hospitality—be always welcoming—without complaining. The early church wouldn't have survived without the hospitality communities provided to traveling missionaries they didn't know. Similarly, we need to extend our welcome to people who are different from us—whether it's because of their culture, their language, their religion, their social status, and so forth—because we are all members of the family of God.

We should use the gifts we have received from God to benefit others: our talents, our homes, our money, our time, our energy, our practical know-how, our artistic sense, our ready sympathy, our life experiences. We are stewards of these gifts; they have been entrusted to us on behalf of others.

In short we should say everything we say, and do everything we do, "so that God may be glorified in all things through Jesus Christ" (1 Peter 4:11). Although quite simple in principle, this sounds like a pretty tall order, because it requires us to put the needs of others and the will of God before our own needs and desires. We don't need to worry, though, for we are to do these things "with the strength that God supplies," because "to him belong the glory and the power forever and ever" (4:11).

"Lord Jesus, give me the strength to ungrudgingly share my love, my hospitality, and my gifts with your children. Help me to put the needs of others before my own and to do everything I do so that you may be glorified."

1 Peter 4:12-19

12 Beloved, do not be surprised at the fiery ordeal that is taking place among you to test you, as though something strange were happening to you. 13But rejoice insofar as you are sharing Christ's sufferings, so that you may also be glad and shout for joy when his glory is revealed. 14If you are reviled for the name of Christ, you are blessed, because the spirit of glory, which is the Spirit of God, is resting on

you. ¹⁵But let none of you suffer as a murderer, a thief, a criminal, or even as a mischief maker. ¹⁶Yet if any of you suffers as a Christian, do not consider it a disgrace, but glorify God because you bear this name. ¹⁷For the time has come for judgment to begin with the household of God; if it begins with us, what will be the end for those who do not obey the gospel of God? ¹⁸And

"If it is hard for the righteous to be saved,
    what will become of the ungodly and the sinners?"
¹⁹Therefore, let those suffering in accordance with God's will entrust themselves to a faithful Creator, while continuing to do good. ✎

When things don't go our way, we easily become disgruntled. Didn't God promise prosperity to those who follow him? "Beloved," chides Peter, "do not be surprised at the fiery ordeal that is taking place among you" (1 Peter 4:12). Because there is some disagreement about the date of this letter, we're not sure if the author was talking about deadly persecution under Emperor Nero, or simply using hyperbole to describe the ridicule and ostracism these gentile converts were experiencing at the hands of former friends and neighbors. But whatever the nature of the original audience's trials, Peter's words point us to the right attitude we all should have if we are faced with similar situations.

We're lucky. We probably won't ever suffer real persecution for our beliefs. Though, there are places in the world where—even today—Christians are being denied their rights, tortured, and even sentenced to death. The only "persecution" we're likely to experience is a general dislike or mistrust of Catholics, which could be the result of anything from a negative experience someone had in Catholic school years ago to a disagreement with the church's stance on reproductive issues. Once people get to know us, however, their view of Catholicism is more likely to be shaped by the way they see us live our faith.

If, for example, we say that we believe in truth, and then cheat on our taxes—what sort of faith are we living? If we say that we believe in justice, and then spread rumors—what sort of faith are we living? And if we say that we are all God's children, and then exclude some people from our circle of friends—what sort of faith are we living?

We are called to be Christ's representatives in the world, which means that our daily lives should reflect what it means to be a Christian. We may in fact be called upon one day to suffer for what we believe. But it's up to us to make sure that we are actually suffering because of our faith, and not because we have let ourselves become smug, self-righteous, or difficult to get along with. As the author of this letter advises, "If you are reviled for the name of Christ, you are blessed," but there is no honor in suffering for our own misdeeds, "or even as a mischief maker" (1 Peter 4:15-16). What a great opportunity to grow in humility, holiness, and dependence on God!

In the meantime, trials will come "to test you," (1 Peter 4:12) to strengthen what you are made of. They can prune away attachments to secondary things and help you refocus on what matters most (John 15:2). Physical and emotional suffering are a natural part of our lives as human beings. When they occur, we can use them to join ourselves to Christ's suffering and offer them for the needs of the world. As St. Paul said, his own suffering would complete "what is lacking in Christ's afflictions for the sake of his body, . . . the church" (Colossians 1:24).

In our earthly lives, we can also expect to experience death. This "death" can take many forms: the end of relationships, the crushing of aspirations, the death of loved ones, sacrifices made out of love, and ultimately, facing our own mortality.

Death, yes, but we can also see resurrections. God is in the business of bringing good out of evil, his glory out of our shame, his victory out of our defeats, and resurrection life out of the darkness of death.

Knowing all this, we can simply "do right and entrust ourselves to a faithful Creator" (1 Peter 4:19). The results are up to God. We may never know what has caused our suffering, or what good purpose it serves in the divine economy. Not having to figure out these things can be very liberating.

"Jesus, thank you for letting me share in some small way in your suffering. Give me your joy in the midst of difficulties so that others may be drawn to your resurrection life."

1 Peter 5:1-5

[1] Now as an elder myself and a witness of the sufferings of Christ, as well as one who shares in the glory to be revealed, I exhort the elders among you [2] to tend the flock of God that is in your charge, exercising the oversight, not under compulsion but willingly, as God would have you do it—not for sordid gain but eagerly. [3] Do not lord it over those in your charge, but be examples to the flock. [4] And when the chief shepherd appears, you will win the crown of glory that never fades away. [5] In the same way, you who are younger must accept the authority of the elders. And all of you must clothe yourselves with humility in your dealings with one another, for

"God opposes the proud,
    but gives grace to the humble."

Here we have a privileged communication from Jesus' first chosen "under-shepherd" to others entrusted with the same pastoral ministry. Pope Peter reminds us that Jesus is the good shepherd; all human authority comes from him and is to be exercised in him. Despite his special position in the church, Peter identifies himself as a fellow "elder" (1 Peter 5:1). He has been privileged to witness Jesus' sufferings—and to have a glimpse of his glory. We know that it wasn't very long before Peter too laid down his life for his sheep by being crucified upside down.

We who are not bishops or pastors may be tempted to skip over this section and see what Peter has to say to us sheep. However, every member of the body of Christ has been entrusted with responsibilities; and with those responsibilities comes authority. The Vatican II document *On the Laity* states this very forcibly: "As sharers in the role of Christ as priest, prophet, and king, the laity have their work cut out for them in the life and activity of the Church. Their activity is so necessary within the Church communities that without it the apostolate of the pastors is often unable to achieve its full effectiveness" (10).

How then shall we exercise our God-given authority as parents, teachers, or leaders of service projects? "Not under compulsion but willingly" (1 Peter 5:2)—not as an onerous duty we take on, making sure everyone knows what a martyr we are, but with genuine gratitude for the opportunity to serve. "Not for sordid gain but eagerly" (5:2)—not for our own benefit, either in the hope of material or heavenly reward, but unselfishly, for the good of those we serve, putting their interests before our own (Philippians 2:4). "Do not lord it over those in your charge, but be examples to the flock" (1 Peter 5:3)—not bullying people into doing the right thing, but leading in a way that draws them into the work with an enthusiasm that will sustain them when the going gets rough.

Moving on to the "flock," Peter exhorts them to "accept the authority of the elders," (1 Peter 5:5) offering their insight as decisions are being made and then following the shepherd's leadership without resentment or complaint.

Peter saves his most important admonition for shepherd and sheep alike: "All of you must clothe yourselves with humility" (1 Peter 5:5)—humility that exalts the Lord and profoundly respects the role of each member of the body: priests and laity, leaders and followers, co-workers all in the body of Christ.

"Thank you, Holy Spirit, for calling and equipping me to serve in the church and in the world as an instrument of your love and truth."

1 Peter 5:6-11

[6] Humble yourselves therefore under the mighty hand of God, so that he may exalt you in due time. [7]Cast all your anxiety on him, because he cares for you. [8]Discipline yourselves, keep alert. Like a roaring lion your adversary the devil prowls around, looking for someone to devour. [9]Resist him, steadfast in your faith, for you know that your brothers and sisters in all the world are undergoing the same kinds of suffering. [10]And after you have suffered for a little while, the God of all grace, who has called you to his eternal glory in Christ, will himself restore, support, strengthen, and establish you. [11]To him be the power forever and ever. Amen.

The low doorway of humility provides the only access to all the other Christian virtues. However, humility is seldom achieved deliberately; focusing on it has the ironic effect of opening us up to pride and self-centeredness. No, humility is a byproduct of following the Lord. Still, Peter gives us several important steps to help us become humble in the right way.

The first is to glorify God. "Humble yourselves therefore under the mighty hand of God. . . . To him be the power for ever and ever. Amen" (1 Peter 5:6, 11). Exalting our Creator doesn't abase us. When we put him in his rightful place, we gain the right perspective on ourselves.

Next, keep God's bright promise in view: "That he may exalt you in due time. . . . After you have suffered for a little while, the God of all grace, who has called you to his eternal glory in Christ, will himself restore, support, strengthen, and establish you" (1 Peter 5:6, 10). When you're in the trenches, it's easy to get bogged down by hard or boring work that doesn't feel like it's achieving anything. Instead, look to the future, seize the big picture, and trust that God is working out greater purposes than you can perceive from your limited perspective.

Then, "Cast all your anxiety on him, because he cares for you" (1 Peter 5:7). Don't be ashamed of admitting concerns and inadequacies and asking God for help. This usually means asking others for help too, for our brothers and sisters also care about us. This is the pathway of humility, rather than pridefully thinking we ought to be able to handle everything by ourselves.

You have a bond with all Christians: "Your brothers and sisters in all the world are undergoing the same kinds of suffering" (1 Peter 5:9). You are not called to be a lone ranger solving the world's problems by yourself, nor do you face any hardships unique to you. Only pride thinks that way.

Why does Peter then bring in the devil? Peter is a realist. He knows from personal experience that Lucifer, who wanted to be equal to God, appeals powerfully to the same pride in us. He wants us to be self-centered, and he seeks to divide us from one another, thus separating us from God. Because the devil tries to undermine our confidence in God, Peter advises firmness in faith as the most effective strategy in defeating him. And what is the shortest path to firm faith? You guessed it: humility!

"Jesus Christ, you humbled yourself to become one with us. Lead me in the path of humility. Open my eyes so that I will be able to identify and resist the devil's temptations to pride."

1 Peter 5:12-14

[12] Through Silvanus, whom I consider a faithful brother, I have written this short letter to encourage you and to testify that this is the true grace of God. Stand fast in it. [13]Your sister church in Babylon, chosen together with you, sends you greetings; and so does my son Mark. [14]Greet one another with a kiss of love.
Peace to all of you who are in Christ.

In these few verses, Peter sums up his message: "This is the true grace of God. Stand fast in it. . . . Peace to all who are in Christ" (1 Peter 5:12, 14). And lest this sound too vague and theoretical, he reminds his audience to "greet one another with a kiss of love" (5:14), genuine affection expressed in bodily form. Holy embraces seem to have been common in the early church, since Paul gives the same directive in 1 Corinthians (16:20) and 1 Thessalonians (5:26).

From general exhortations, Peter moves to news of and from particular individuals and communities, greetings from the church at "Babylon," that is, Rome, "chosen" (1 Peter 5:13) to suffer and to give glory to Jesus Christ.

Peter's companions, Silvanus (Silas) and Mark, have a long history together. Both belonged to the first Christian community in

Jerusalem, where they got to know Peter. Mark's home was the place where the church gathered to pray that Peter would be released from prison (Acts 12:12). Silas was one of the elders chosen to bring word to the mixed Jewish gentile community at Antioch about the apostles' decision that gentile converts did not need to keep the whole Mosaic law (15:22).

Both Mark and Silas were missionary companions of St. Paul, but not under the most amicable conditions. Mark accompanied Paul and Barnabas on their first journey but evidently became homesick and deserted them (Acts 13:13). When it was time to embark on a second evangelistic trip, Barnabas wanted to give Mark a second chance, but Paul wouldn't hear of it. After a "sharp disagreement" (15:39), Paul enlisted Silas to go with him in one direction while Barnabas and Mark went in another. This effectively doubled the impact of the gospel, and evidently Mark was so faithful in this endeavor that he earned his way back into Paul's good graces; the apostle identified him in Philemon 24 as "among his fellow workers."

From their checkered history with Paul, Silas and Mark became close companions to Peter. In fact, such close association with Peter probably provided much of the material Mark drew on in writing his gospel. Perhaps he was able to recount Peter's betrayal and repentance (Mark 14:66-72) with such feeling by drawing on his own personal experience of being forgiven and given a second chance. God seems to delight in interweaving Christian friends' lives, bringing us back together as co-workers who can draw on our common heritage, as well as our particular experiences. May the same be true for us as we digest all that Peter has taught us in this letter. May grace flow to all who are bound together by the common bond of baptism!

"Lord, thank you for giving me co-workers in your body whose talents complement those you have given me. Help me be quick to forgive and encourage, believing the best about each brother and sister."

BAPTIZED INTO A NEW DIGNITY

84

Living in the Shadow of the "Day of the Lord"

The Second Letter of Peter

Living in the Shadow of the "Day of the Lord"

An Introduction to the Second Letter of Peter

Rev. Henry Wansbrough, OSB

The Second Letter of Peter—one of the latest New Testament letters—introduces us to the world of the church at the end of the first century. By the time this letter was written, many of the first generation of Christians had died, and their successors were left wondering whatever happened to the promised second coming. This is precisely the issue that 2 Peter tackles. In it, the author warns his readers against growing slack or careless because they think that Jesus' return is not imminent—or that it may not happen at all. An ominous air of doom pervades the letter: "The heavens will be set ablaze and dissolved, and the elements will melt with fire," he warns (2 Peter 3:12). At the same time, "we wait for new heavens and a new earth" (3:13).

It is as if the author is cautioning his readers against thinking that there will be no day of reckoning. He reminds them that God has caused disastrous judgments in the past, including the fall of the rebellious angels, the flood, and the destruction of Sodom and Gomorrah (2 Peter 2:4-6). Plus, the divine time-scale is different from ours: to God a day is like a thousand years, and a thousand years are like a day. The day of the Lord will come suddenly and unexpectedly, "like a thief" (3:10).

Sandwiched between these two arguments is interspersed a sparkling diatribe—perhaps the most rhetorical and vehement in the whole of the New Testament—against false teachers who seek to lead the faithful astray. The accusations of moral corruption leveled against these teachers should, perhaps, not be taken too seriously; they were standard accusations made against teachers whose doctrine a writer considered erroneous.

The Atmosphere of 2 Peter. The atmosphere of 2 Peter is that of a farewell letter, instructions to his followers from a leader who is about to depart. The greeting at the beginning follows the standard opening of a letter in the ancient world (and with the touchingly personal Hebrew form of the name "Simeon" instead of the Greek "Simon"). But that is where the letter formula stops. It does not continue in any way to resemble a letter, and there is not even a standard "signing off" at the end.

Instead, 2 Peter is best compared with other "farewell instructions" in the New Testament. The best known and most important is Jesus' long discourse at the Last Supper in John 14-17. Other examples include Paul's speech to the elders of Ephesus in Acts 20 and the Second Letter to Timothy. In 2 Peter, the author acknowledges that his death "will come soon" (2 Peter 1:14). Consequently, he is determined to keep his followers on the right path, despite the false teachers and their private interpretations of scriptural prophecy (1:20). In contrast to these self-important "prophets," the author gently hints at his own right to offer guidance. He had himself been a witness of the transfiguration, "while we were with him on the holy mountain" (1:18). He also makes the point that this is the second letter he has written to them (3:1), and links arms with "our beloved brother Paul" (3:15), despite the difficulty he finds in understanding his letters.

Who Is "Peter"? Even though personal notes are struck by these passages and appear to link the author with St. Peter, it is hard to believe that the fisherman Peter himself penned the letter. Sophisticated literary figures abound, such as the sorites (literally "heap":

A → B, B → C, C → D, etc.) in 2 Peter 1:5-7; the energetic and bizarre comparison of the false teachers to "irrational animals, mere creatures of instinct, born to be caught and killed" and to "waterless springs and mists driven by a storm" (2:12, 17); not to mention the colorful abusive proverbs such as "The sow is washed only to wallow in the mud" (2:22). These are all examples of a Greek style known as "Asian rhetoric" because most examples of it stem from writers of Asia Minor and east of the Mediterranean.

Likewise, the virtues that the author insists his readers embrace are not phrased in the classic "gospel" style but are the virtues typical of the Greek world and of the popular Stoic philosophy: knowledge, self-control, endurance, and love of brothers (1:6-7). Moreover, the Greek names for these virtues make the difference of the thought-world all the sharper. Clearly, we are no longer in the simple atmosphere of the Galilean lakeside.

At the same time, however, the author is clearly steeped in the Jewish tradition. For instance, he uses the precedents of Jewish history, drawn from nonbiblical Jewish writings (2:4-6), to help make his case. These precedents must have been well known in Jewish Christian circles, since they are also used in the Letter of Jude. Such a technique—and even the stories the author recalls—bulked large in Jewish moral writings of the time.

The Date of the Letter. One factor that helps us better understand the nature of this letter is the probable date. A century ago, wild attempts were made to date 2 Peter as late as A.D. 150. Such attempts have now ceased. It was certainly written well before the noncanonical *Apocalypse of Peter*, dated to A.D. 130. Responsible scholarly opinion today places it near the end of the first century A.D.

The disappointment (or overconfidence, in the case of those recipients who are being warned) that the second coming hadn't happened points to a gap in time since the resurrection and the vivid expectation of Paul's letters. This is probably the meaning also of "ever since our ancestors [literally, "fathers"] died" (2 Peter 3:4), which suggests that the first generation of Christians has, at least mostly, died away.

The general comment about the wisdom that Paul shows "in all his letters" (2 Peter 3:16) suggests that his letters were available in what seemed to be a total collection. By contrast, the Acts of the Apostles, written possibly in the eighties, shows no awareness that Paul even wrote letters, let alone that they had been collected.

As for a date before which 2 Peter must have been written, the social stability and steadiness of the letter, the frequent condemnation of "lawlessness," and the respect for authority that pervade the letter would be less likely after the virulent persecution sponsored by the Emperor Diocletian in his final two years (A.D. 94–96). There is no word at all of bloodshed or persecution, and both the writer and his community seem peacefully settled in society. The whole atmosphere of the letter is very similar to that of a letter written by Clement of Rome to the Corinthians in the early nineties. Apparently, this would be a suitable date for 2 Peter as well.

The Author. Who, then, wrote the letter? The date as well as the tone make it highly unlikely that Peter the apostle himself literally wrote it. By the final decade of the century he would have been very old indeed by the standards of the day. The reference to "our beloved brother Paul" would also be a little unlikely in view of the full-scale row Peter and Paul had at Antioch (Galatians 2:11-14), after which each went his own way, without any sign of reconciliation. If Peter entrusted the writing to a secretary and merely oversaw the writing or authorized the finished product, we have seen that the thought diverges so much from what we know of Peter's own way of thinking that he can only have given a very general impetus to the writing.

It seems more suitable to invoke the concept of "pseudepigraphy." This means that the letter was written by someone other than Peter and was presented as Peter's, because the author considered that this was what Peter *would have said* in such a situation. This convention was so common in the first century that there was no question of deception. The *Psalms of Solomon*, included in the Greek translation of the Old Testament, are noble prayers of the Pharisaic tradition in the first century before Christ—certainly not authored by Solomon. Numerous writings of the first century are also attributed to Enoch, who, according to Genesis 5:24, "walked with God" until "God took him." Because of this he was considered the special revealer of God's ways; and the revelations of the Books of Enoch were widespread and revered in the Jewish world.

In the New Testament itself, the pastoral letters addressed to Timothy and Titus are so different in style, approach, and theology that many scholars believe that they must have been written by someone in touch with Paul who reckoned what Paul *would have written* in such a situation. In a similar way, it is reasonable to assume that an unknown, inspired author wrote what he reckoned Peter *would have written* to reorient these straying Christians.

The Second Coming. At its heart, 2 Peter issues a challenge to readers to reach an understanding of what Christians believe about the second coming of Christ. In 1 Thessalonians 4:15-16, Paul seems to expect a coming of Christ on the clouds of heaven within a generation. The crisis at Thessalonika arose because the Thessalonian Christians mistakenly understood Paul's teaching that Christ had conquered death to mean that Christians would not die before the second coming. Furthermore, Paul's teaching on celibacy and child-lessness in 1 Corinthians 7 assumes that the agonizing turmoil of the final days will occur very soon.

So vivid is the expectation of Jesus' return that one of the very few Aramaic phrases retained in the Greek of the New Testament is *Maranatha*, "Our Lord, come!" (1 Corinthians 16:22). Similarly, the Gospel of Mark (especially Mark 13, but also such passages as 9:1 and 14:62), written perhaps a dozen years after 1 Corinthians, can also be interpreted as associating the destruction of Jerusalem in A.D. 70 with an immediate second coming of Christ.

Later gospels tone down this expectation. Luke explicitly dis-sociates the sack of Jerusalem from the second coming. He still shows Jesus teaching about a coming on the clouds of heaven (Luke 21:27), but adjusts the saying at Jesus' trial to exclude any mention of the "clouds." Instead, Jesus says simply, "From now on the Son of Man will be seated at the right hand of the power of God" (22:69). In Acts 1:7, the risen Christ tells his disciples, "It is not for you to know the times or periods that the Father has set by his own author-ity." And in John, there is no mention at all of a second coming at the end of time.

Now, in 2 Peter, the writer clearly expects the last days (2 Peter 3:3), a day of judgment (3:7), and a day of the Lord when the uni-verse will be dissolved with fire (3:10, 12). While the letter does not explicitly mention a second coming, it's important to see that the denial of such an event is attributed to "scoffers" and not to true believers (3:3). But on the timing of this event, the key is "with the Lord one day is like a thousand years, and a thousand years are like one day" (3:8). Clearly, there has been a development in the think-ing on this matter in the course of the New Testament, with 2 Peter representing a later development.

How Shall We Live? Today, we are centuries and centuries away from the first Christians and their expectation of an immediate return of Christ. Many of the questions they faced seem remote from us. Many of their assumptions sound as if they were sealed in a time capsule. But one question remains constant: "Since all these things are to be dissolved in this way, what sort of people ought you to be in leading lives of holiness and godliness?" (2 Peter 3:11). The second coming is not a myth. Jesus will return to judge the living and the dead. So how can we best prepare for that day? And just as the question remains the same, the answer remains the same as well: "Strive to be found by him at peace, without spot or blemish" (3:14). May the Lord fill us with the hope, perseverance, and patience that this letter urges upon us. May we never lose sight of the salvation he has promised to us all.

2 Peter 1:1-8

¹ Simeon Peter, a servant and apostle of Jesus Christ,

To those who have received a faith as precious as ours through the righteousness of our God and Savior Jesus Christ:
² May grace and peace be yours in abundance in the knowledge of God and of Jesus our Lord.
³ His divine power has given us everything needed for life and godliness, through the knowledge of him who called us by his own glory and goodness. ⁴Thus he has given us, through these things, his precious and very great promises, so that through them you may escape from the corruption that is in the world because of lust, and may become participants of the divine nature. ⁵For this very reason, you must make every effort to support your faith with goodness, and goodness with knowledge, ⁶and knowledge with self-control, and self-control with endurance, and endurance with godliness, ⁷and godliness with mutual affection, and mutual affection with love. ⁸For if these things are yours and are increasing among you, they keep you from being ineffective and unfruitful in the knowledge of our Lord Jesus Christ.

Have you ever noticed how easy it can be to reduce Christianity to a set of rules for successful living? But such a vision falls short of the glorious calling that God has for each one of us. Scripture tells us that God's purpose is that we be so conformed to Christ that we actually become "participants of the divine nature" (2 Peter 1:4). St. Augustine once asked, "What greater grace could God have made to dawn on us than to make his only Son become the son of man, so that a son of man might in his turn become son of God?" (Sermon 185).

Peter lays out the steps we can take that will keep us in touch with this great gift of the divine nature active in our hearts: supporting our faith with goodness, knowledge, self-control, endurance, godliness, and brotherly love (2 Peter 1:5-7). The promise holds just as true today as it did back then: "If you do this . . . entry into the eternal kingdom of our Lord and Savior Jesus Christ will be richly provided for you" (1:10-11).

The question we must always ask ourselves is whether we are keeping Jesus at the center of our journey. If our vision of Christianity is limited to personal, moral, or financial success, then we will only strive for a peaceful existence on earth—a kind of responsible love for ourselves, our families, and perhaps our communities. Of course, these are good things, but they reduce the gospel message and are only a part of what God wants for us.

More than anything else, the gospel has to do with God's inviting us into his very life—his invitation that we become one with Jesus, through whom and for whom everything was made. When we put the presence of Christ above every other concern, all of our efforts will become successful. Let us allow the Holy Spirit to bring us to Jesus. Let us expand our vision and embrace Jesus. As we do, our every effort will be magnified for God's glory.

"Father, I praise you for the excellency of Jesus' life and death. In all of heaven and earth there is no one greater. We cry out today for his presence to fill our lives."

2 Peter 1:9-15

[9]For anyone who lacks these things is nearsighted and blind, and is forgetful of the cleansing of past sins. [10]Therefore, brothers and sisters, be all the more eager to confirm your call and election, for if you do this, you will never stumble. [11]For in this way, entry into the

eternal kingdom of our Lord and Savior Jesus Christ will be richly provided for you.

[12] Therefore I intend to keep on reminding you of these things, though you know them already and are established in the truth that has come to you. [13]I think it right, as long as I am in this body, to refresh your memory, [14]since I know that my death will come soon, as indeed our Lord Jesus Christ has made clear to me. [15]And I will make every effort so that after my departure you may be able at any time to recall these things. 🖎

I intend to keep on reminding you of these things. (2 Peter 1:12)

I magine a mother saying for the tenth time that day, "pick up your clothes" or "do your homework," or a coach telling a young soccer player again and again to keep her eye on the ball. Anyone who knows children knows that they often have to be reminded repeatedly to stay on the right track and continue to do what they have already been taught.

Now back up a couple of thousand years to see Peter, anticipating his execution and thinking about the church that he has given his life to serve. Like any good father, Peter's heart was filled with concern for the people under his care. He wanted them to be steadfast in the faith, recalling all the things they had learned. And so Peter resolved to keep reminding these children in the Lord of all that he had taught them.

When we go to church, we may feel like we keep hearing the same things over and over again. The gospel readings repeat every few years; even the homilies may seem redundant. But is that always a bad thing? Or is this perhaps just another way that God wants to keep the heart of the gospel fresh in our memories? The repetition can be a real help to us, opening up opportunities to go deeper into the understanding we already have!

For instance, the accounts of Jesus' passion, death, and resurrection are read several times during Lent and Easter. We may dread the long gospels on those days. But what about using these repeated readings to pray more deeply about Jesus' suffering and the new life he has poured upon you? How about trying to place yourself in the story, imagining how you would have responded if you were Peter, Mary, or even Pontius Pilate? Jesus has so much to tell us, that we will never be able to exhaust the Scriptures. We will never come to the bottom of the depths of knowledge of Christ—and love for him—that they offer!

Let's see how we can respond when God keeps reminding us of the central truths of the gospel. Who knows? Maybe we will experience a breakthrough we never expected, or a deeper insight that lifts up our hearts and heals our memories.

"Heavenly Father, thank you for the inexhaustible depths of Scripture! Thank you for constantly reminding me to return to your word for understanding. May we never come to the end of your goodness and mercy!"

2 Peter 1:16-18

[16] For we did not follow cleverly devised myths when we made known to you the power and coming of our Lord Jesus Christ, but we had been eyewitnesses of his majesty. [17]For he received honor and glory from God the Father when that voice was conveyed to him by the Majestic Glory, saying, "This is my Son, my Beloved, with whom I am well pleased." [18]We ourselves heard this voice come from heaven, while we were with him on the holy mountain.

I magine for a moment that you're out hiking and discover an old canal tunnel. You've never been in one before and decide to hike through to the other side.

At first, the going is easy, as the light from the entrance illuminates the narrow walking path and the deep canal to your left. As you venture farther, however, the light slowly disappears until you are walking in total darkness. Unable to see, and dangerously close to the invisible drop, you creep forward slowly but steadily, straining for any glimpse of light to ease your growing sense of uncertainty. The knowledge that light will eventually be visible is the only thing that keeps you moving through the unbroken darkness. You can only look straight ahead and try to conquer your rising sense of fear.

After what seems like hours, a point of light appears in the distance—the other end of the tunnel! You breathe a deep sigh of relief as you safely make your way out of the darkness and into daylight once again.

Peter told his readers that the transfiguration of Jesus was like "a lamp shining in a dark place, until the day dawns and the morning star rises" in our hearts (2 Peter 1:19). Peter knew that the vision of Jesus transfigured in all his glory plus the words of his Father's approval can give us great hope in a world filled with danger and uncertainty. When we cannot see where we are going or how we will get through, Jesus stands with his hands stretched out to us, asking to let his light illuminate our hearts.

Brothers and sisters, the transfiguration tells us that Jesus Christ has conquered sin and death! Following him, we *will* share in his victory! He has promised to be with us always and to bring us to be with his Father forever. No darkness can ever be too deep for Jesus to illuminate, for he is the King of Kings and Lord of Lords.

"Jesus, you are so faithful! Never once have you left me alone. Thank you for always being my light in a dark world."

2 Peter 1:19-21

[19] So we have the prophetic message more fully confirmed. You will do well to be attentive to this as to a lamp shining in a dark place, until the day dawns and the morning star rises in your hearts. [20]First of all you must understand this, that no prophecy of scripture is a matter of one's own interpretation, [21]because no prophecy ever came by human will, but men and women moved by the Holy Spirit spoke from God.

Have you ever noticed how difficult it is to figure out exactly what happened in a politically charged situation? Maybe the senator illegally took funds from an interested lobbying group. Or, maybe he was totally within his legal rights, and all the challenges are political smear tactics. There seem to be two sides to every story, and whoever is better at "finessing" the story ends up with more support. Public opinion gets swayed, and the truth is often left fuzzy.

When you approach God's word, do you sometimes feel the same way? You might hear different preachers highlight different points of Scripture and arrive at different conclusions. How can you approach such a daunting task as understanding God's word, when there seems to be so much room for interpretation?

Peter reminds us that God's word cannot be "finessed" to suit our purposes; his truth is not swayed by public opinion. When the heavenly Father identified Jesus as his beloved Son, he didn't leave any loopholes. Similarly, you won't see the church taking opinion polls to help it identify and define moral questions. And while Jesus often spoke in parables, and the Scriptures contain much figurative language, still the truth of the gospel remains the same even today.

In fact, Jesus wants his gospel to be a beacon that gives us direction even when other things might be unclear. He wants us to know that God's word is a sure foundation, something that can withstand the forces of changing times and opinions—even if those opinions are our own! When we feel tossed by uncertainty, we should go back to the truths that we know: Jesus loves us personally; he died so that our sins could be forgiven and we could spend eternity with him in heaven; he sent his Holy Spirit to dwell in us and guide us; he will come again in glory to restore all things to himself. When we keep our eyes fixed on this beacon of truth, we will be able to sort out the other areas that are unclear. The church offers us immense help, providing an unchanging, stable foundation for every aspect of our lives.

It is immensely important—and amazingly refreshing—to seek to understand the unchanging truth that is in God's word. So let the unchanging light of the gospel show you the way to walk, and every step will bring you closer and closer to Jesus.

"Lord, thank you that you never change. Your words are just as relevant today as they were thousands of years ago. Your promises never fade, and your truth never darkens. You are my sure foundation!"

2 Peter 2:1-3

¹ But false prophets also arose among the people, just as there will be false teachers among you, who will secretly bring in destructive opinions. They will even deny the Master who bought them—bringing swift destruction on themselves. ²Even so, many will follow their licentious ways, and because of these teachers the way of truth will be maligned. ³And in their greed they will exploit you with deceptive words. Their condemnation, pronounced against them long ago, has not been idle, and their destruction is not asleep. ☙

There will be false teachers among you. (2 Peter 2:1)

What? Is Peter saying that we should expect false teachers? That we should not be surprised to see people promoting contrary doctrines, even denying Jesus? And that these people, drawing followers, will malign the church in the eyes of the world? How can he be so detached?

Peter knew human nature. He had seen a lot in his life, and you get the feeling that nothing surprised him. Of course, people motivated by greed and the desire for power will try to redefine what it means to follow Christ, along with redefining what is acceptable or moral. And of course, some people will be deceived into following their teachings. Their situation in the eyes of God is dire, and he alone can judge them; in the interim, the church will suffer from their influence.

We can all think of examples of such false teachers in our present day, people who change the teaching of the gospel. And we can probably see the effects as well: people ridiculing or discrediting believers or the church itself; and worse, people being exploited, led down a path away from the truth, comfort, and salvation found in Christ.

When you look at it this way, it really can be hard to be as unemotional as Peter seems. So what was his secret? Peter could see the end of the story. He knew that God's justice would prevail, even if that justice was not fully visible in the present moment. Peter knew that the choices made by those leading others astray, assuming they did not repent, would eventually end in destruction. He knew that the gates of hell would never prevail against the church!

We can make the decision to embrace that same hope for the church, even when we see things that make us feel hopeless. Like Peter, our hope can be like a house built on a rock, unshaken despite wind and storm. We know the end of the story, and Jesus will restore his church to share his glory.

"Jesus, you love your church! I praise you, Lord, for promising never to abandon your people. May I never forget this amazing truth."

2 Peter 2:4-11

[4] For if God did not spare the angels when they sinned, but cast them into hell and committed them to chains of deepest darkness to be kept until the judgment; [5]and if he did not spare the ancient world, even though he saved Noah, a herald of righteousness, with seven others, when he brought a flood on a world of the ungodly; [6]and if by turning the cities of Sodom and Gomorrah to ashes he condemned them to extinction and made them an example of what is coming to the ungodly; [7]and if he rescued Lot, a righteous man greatly distressed by the licentiousness of the lawless [8](for that righteous man, living among them day after day, was tormented in his righteous soul by their lawless deeds that he saw and heard), [9]then the Lord knows how to rescue the godly from trial, and to keep the unrighteous under punishment until the day of judgment [10]—especially those who indulge their flesh in depraved lust, and who despise authority.

Bold and willful, they are not afraid to slander the glorious ones, [11]whereas angels, though greater in might and power, do not bring against them a slanderous judgment from the Lord.

Just look at the world today! Political corruption, sexual disorder, greed, murder! What will happen to us? Wouldn't it be better if God would just take us out of here? Many of us feel that way when we read the newspaper or watch the evening news, or even simply look around our neighborhoods or families. There seems to be so much in our world that is opposed to God and the life we want to live as his followers.

But consider Noah and Lot. They lived in times of desperate evil. God chose to "rescue" them, but not before he used them as examples to those around them. Peter calls Noah a "herald of righteousness," (2 Peter 2:5) and describes Lot living among the ungodly, even though "tormented in his righteous soul" (2:8). God didn't remove them from a sinful environment immediately; he allowed them to live in it as an example of godliness.

Can we be heralds of righteousness in our world? The mere fact that we try to love Jesus and follow him stands in stark contrast to many; but the Holy Spirit might be asking us to take an extra step of witnessing to our faith so that we will be like a light in the darkness. Just as Lot was willing to turn his back on the evil in Sodom and Gomorrah, God is asking us to turn away from enticements to embrace worldly attitudes of right and wrong. Just as Noah risked ridicule by building his huge ark, there are times when we too should risk ridicule by standing up for truth of the gospel when someone maligns it or denies it.

God sees into the heart of every person alive in the world today. He knows those who love him, and he wants them to make a positive difference in the world. The influence of believers is essential in turning the tide of evil; if nothing else, we can at least make sure that others have seen what a follower of Christ looks like. And in the end, we don't need to be afraid. The Lord has a heavenly home for us when our time on this earth is done. He will protect us from all unrighteousness and bring us into his glory if only we hold fast to him!

"Holy Spirit, help me to be an influence of righteousness in the world. Empower me to fulfill my role as an ambassador for Christ, bringing him into every situation I face. Spirit, I want to be a light in the darkness!"

2 Peter 2:12-22

[12]These people, however, are like irrational animals, mere creatures of instinct, born to be caught and killed. They slander what they do not understand, and when those creatures are destroyed, they also will be destroyed, [13]suffering the penalty for doing wrong. They count it a pleasure to revel in the daytime. They are blots and blemishes, reveling in their dissipation while they feast with you. [14]They have eyes full of adultery, insatiable for sin. They entice unsteady souls. They have hearts trained in greed. Accursed children! [15]They have left the straight road and have gone astray, following the road of Balaam son of Bosor, who loved the wages of doing wrong, [16]but was rebuked for his own transgression; a speechless donkey spoke with a human voice and restrained the prophet's madness.

[17] These are waterless springs and mists driven by a storm; for them the deepest darkness has been reserved. [18]For they speak bombastic nonsense, and with licentious desires of the flesh they entice people who have just escaped from those who live in error. [19]They promise them freedom, but they themselves are slaves of corruption; for people are slaves to whatever masters them. [20]For if, after they have escaped the defilements of the world through the knowledge of our Lord and Savior Jesus Christ, they are again entangled in them and overpowered, the last state has become worse for them than the first. [21]For it would have been better for them never to have known the way of righteousness than, after knowing it, to turn back from the

holy commandment that was passed on to them. ²²It has happened
to them according to the true proverb,

"The dog turns back to its own vomit,"

and,

"The sow is washed only to wallow in the mud."

L et's face it. Sin can be very enticing. We can easily slip into
the rationalization that it's OK to do whatever we think will
make us happy—whether it's cheating on our income tax,
experimenting with drugs or alcohol, or having an "innocent fling."
Why can we be drawn to these kinds of things? Because most of the
time, sin promises us something we all want: freedom.

But it's a false promise. Sin doesn't make us free. It enslaves us.
Peter put it best when he wrote that "people are slaves to whatever
masters them" (2 Peter 2:19). For a while, we may feel satisfied by sinful choices, but in time they show themselves to be empty, and even
poisonous to our well being. So how do we get ourselves out from
under the mastery of sin? Only Jesus can set us free. And he offers this
freedom constantly through the Sacrament of Reconciliation.

Through repentance and reconciliation, we can come in contact
with Jesus and receive his forgiveness. The bonds of sin that have
wrapped themselves around us are broken! Even more, reconciliation
offers us the chance to start again and to turn from those things that
promise us false freedom. Jesus gives us the power to say no to sin and
yes to the fulfilling life he offers us as children of God.

The more frequently we receive this powerful source of God's
grace, the easier it will be for us to see sin for what it truly is: a deceptive promise that cuts us off from God, the true source of all that we
really need and desire. The better we know Jesus, the more capable
we become of avoiding the counterfeit happiness promised by sin.

Even when we fall—which we all will from time to time—Jesus

never stops calling us back to himself. He never stops offering his forgiveness. The beauty of divine mercy is that it always invites us to return and receive true freedom. It is a never-ending testimony to the true freedom that is available to all of us, no matter how dark or numerous our sins may seem.

"Lord, open my eyes to all the ways I have enslaved myself to the false promises of sin. Help me to turn to you and receive your mercy. I want to live a new life, free and fulfilled in you!"

2 Peter 3:1-12

1 This is now, beloved, the second letter I am writing to you; in them I am trying to arouse your sincere intention by reminding you ²that you should remember the words spoken in the past by the holy prophets, and the commandment of the Lord and Savior spoken through your apostles. ³First of all you must understand this, that in the last days scoffers will come, scoffing and indulging their own lusts ⁴and saying, "Where is the promise of his coming? For ever since our ancestors died, all things continue as they were from the beginning of creation!" ⁵They deliberately ignore this fact, that by the word of God heavens existed long ago and an earth was formed out of water and by means of water, ⁶through which the world of that time was deluged with water and perished. ⁷But by the same word the present heavens and earth have been reserved for fire, being kept until the day of judgment and destruction of the godless.

8 But do not ignore this one fact, beloved, that with the Lord one day is like a thousand years, and a thousand years are like one day. ⁹The Lord is not slow about his promise, as some think of slowness, but is patient with you, not wanting any to perish, but all to come to repentance. ¹⁰But the day of the Lord will come like a thief, and

then the heavens will pass away with a loud noise, and the elements will be dissolved with fire, and the earth and everything that is done on it will be disclosed.
¹¹ Since all these things are to be dissolved in this way, what sort of persons ought you to be in leading lives of holiness and godliness, ¹²waiting for and hastening the coming of the day of God, because of which the heavens will be set ablaze and dissolved, and the elements will melt with fire? ❧

Y ou can probably picture a businessman or businesswoman, planner in hand, briefcase filled with projects, talking on a cell phone while running to his or her next meeting. Multi-tasking, efficiency, and getting the job done have been elevated to the status of heroic virtues in modern society. Sometimes, getting a job done *quickly* seems more important than doing it *well*. We lose patience with people who don't respond immediately to our requests, and we get frustrated when we can't make something happen on our timetable. In this world of high-speed Internet and instant messaging, the very concept of waiting has become alien to us.

So as Christians, what do we think about waiting for Jesus to return? In our task-oriented world, we may be tempted to question why it hasn't already happened. Is Jesus really coming again, or is the second coming just some figurative teaching? Since everything seems to be going along just as it has been for millennia, maybe he doesn't really care. If he is really interested in our world, why hasn't he intervened already? What's taking him so long?

God sees things very differently than we do. He doesn't look at the sweep of human history as if it were a timetable. To a certain degree, the passage of a certain number of days is irrelevant to him; what he cares about is the condition of the soul of each person on earth. His delay is not disinterest but mercy and patience. In love for us, God gives us more time. He wants every person to come to repentance and be ready for his return!

While we wait for Jesus' return, we can take advantage of the mercy that is offered to us. Despite our desire to be in control, we can begin to understand that sometimes the outcome is beyond our reach, the timetable is beyond our control. Waiting isn't necessarily bad; it gives us the time to grow in knowledge and love of Jesus, to make sure we are doing all we can to be ready, so that Jesus will find us looking for him when he comes.

So instead of feeling impatient, we should thank God for his mercy and patience. Let's pray today for the grace to see our lives—and all of history—from his loving perspective.

"Thank you, Lord, that you are not like us! You offer us mercy instead of rushing to judgment. Help me to see that your mercy is for me, and embolden me to take advantage of it today!"

2 Peter 3:13-18

[13]But, in accordance with his promise, we wait for new heavens and a new earth, where righteousness is at home.
[14] Therefore, beloved, while you are waiting for these things, strive to be found by him at peace, without spot or blemish; [15]and regard the patience of our Lord as salvation. So also our beloved brother Paul wrote to you according to the wisdom given him, [16]speaking of this as he does in all his letters. There are some things in them hard to understand, which the ignorant and unstable twist to their own destruction, as they do the other scriptures. [17]You therefore, beloved, since you are forewarned, beware that you are not carried away with the error of the lawless and lose your own stability. [18]But grow in the grace and knowledge of our Lord and

Savior Jesus Christ. To him be the glory both now and to the day of eternity. Amen. ⤳

When a young man becomes engaged, it isn't unusual for him to spend even more time with his fiancée than before. Indeed, it would seem strange if, once they were engaged, he suddenly began to spend less and less time with her. It would be even stranger if he started dating other women!

It would be just as strange if, once we come to know Jesus' love and presence in our lives, we begin spending more time with his rivals. Jesus wants us to see his second coming as the consummation of our relationship with him, as our wedding day when we will finally be united with him in an unbreakable bond of love. So, as we are looking forward to this day, shouldn't we try to be with him and want to please him more than ever? Shouldn't we put aside the other loves that want to draw us away from him?

This is why Peter encouraged his readers to "strive to be found by him at peace, without spot or blemish" (2 Peter 3:14). Peter wasn't trying to frighten them into holiness. God doesn't want us to live righteous lives out of fear of judgment. The Scriptures make it clear that heaven is ours because Jesus shed his blood, not because we have averted God's wrath by doing all the right things.

The question then arises: if we don't get into heaven because of our works, but because of Jesus' love, then why should we put forth any effort? For the same reason a man stays faithful to his fiancée: because of love. Jesus' love for us is so fulfilling that we don't want to do anything that would compromise our relationship with him. Because the allures of this fallen world pale in comparison, and separate us from him, we know we should avoid them.

Peter knew that whenever we tolerate or remain comfortable with sin, it's because we misunderstand the nature and depth of

God's love. Almighty God, who owes us nothing but has given us everything in Christ, is jealous for our love. Let us find within our hearts a deep desire to love him exclusively in return.

"Jesus, how I long for your return! By your Spirit, empower me to minister your love to others as I wait for you with hope and longing. Come, Lord Jesus!"

Living in the Shadow of the "Day of the Lord"

Walking in the Light of Truth

The First Letter of John

WALKING IN THE LIGHT OF TRUTH

Walking in the Light of Truth
An Introduction to the First Letter of John

Rev. Joseph A. Mindling, OFM Cap

The first of the Johannine epistles, often referred to simply as "1 John," is a powerful combination of personal testimony, apostolic teaching, and urgent exhortation. It was written by a zealous shepherd of souls, very conscious of his role as a teacher as he wrote to a community troubled by dissensions that touched upon the very essentials of their Christian faith.

Although the ancient copyists who preserved this letter consistently attributed it to an otherwise unspecified "John," the text itself never names its author. The fact that more than one early Christian leader bore this same name has allowed some modern scholars to propose various "Johns" as the possible author. Nevertheless, major ancient authorities—like Irenaeus, Clement, Origen, and Tertullian—were substantially unanimous in ascribing this writing to the Beloved Disciple, whom they identified as the author of the fourth gospel and the "John" who is included in all the lists of the twelve apostles found in the New Testament.

The high number of parallels and echoes between the language of this epistle and of the Gospel According to John add further weight to this claim. Although shorter than the gospel, 1 John also speaks in terms of light and darkness, life and truth, the physical reality of the incarnation, and other well-known "Johannine" ideas. This language is not found in any other writings except those that the best manuscripts of the New Testament also connect with the name "John" (Revelation; 2 and 3 John).

The First Recipients and Their Situation. Ancient authorities have identified the recipients of this letter as a Christian community in or around Ephesus (located on the western coast of what is now Turkey). This is where John is said to have fulfilled Jesus' injunction from the cross that he and the Virgin Mary should care for one another. It is also believed to be the place where John continued to preach the gospel during the second half of the first century. Moreover, Paul's Letter to the Ephesians points to the presence of a Christian church in this same area—probably two or three decades before the circumstances that the present letter addresses.

The First Letter of John touches on theologically profound and thought-provoking issues, but not in the form of an academic treatise. Instead, it was written in response to a tense, complex situation that John considered both perilous and urgent because it threatened the faith of those who were still loyal to the beliefs he had shared with them.

This pastoral assessment of the situation made him eager, first of all, to encourage those under his care to protect their privileged friendship with Jesus. This, after all, was the key to eternal life! John was also concerned to protect his people from two dangers that threatened this relationship: first, a worrisome loss of enthusiasm in their commitment as Christians, and second, certain distortions in their understanding of the moral demands of the gospel.

The Content and Message. This letter occupies only four or five pages in a modern translation of the Bible, but its thought is compact. Although it uses a basically simple vocabulary, its sometimes repetitive style is difficult to reduce to a concise summary. It can be challenging for modern readers to follow its thought flow, but with a little time and attention, we will find this to be a very thought-provoking piece of writing.

The letter can be divided into three thematic sections, prefaced with a brief introduction and crowned with an "appendix" that repeats some of John's most pressing concerns. As you read the "mini-commentary" that follows, try to imagine yourself gathered with friends and fellow believers to hear this letter and to discuss how its message applies to you, both personally and as a member of your faith community.

The Preamble: Life Itself Made Visible (1:1-4). Although ancient letters customarily began with a stylized opening (the name of the sender, the intended recipients, and a short blessing), that section is missing here. Instead, we are immediately confronted with two striking declarations.

First, we hear the voice of one of the few persons in history who could speak about Jesus on the basis of a personal and physical contact: "life itself made visible." Second—and this assertion is as striking as the first—John insists that the intimacy he experienced both with Jesus and the Father is within everyone's grasp—in fact, he is eager to help us experience the joy that it brings.

Seeing God as a Healing Light (1:5-10). John calls to mind Jesus' teaching that God is light. Religious traditions throughout history have connected the experience of "light" with the revelation of spiritual mysteries and with the wisdom needed to embrace these mysteries. Light also represents what is morally good, thus adding a claim on our wills and not just on our minds. By contrast, darkness represents not just falsehood but evil and sin—including the sin we find in our personal lives.

To deny that we are sinners is to reject the truth about ourselves that God's light reveals to us. In effect, this amounts to calling God a liar. On the contrary, a frank admission of our sin and of our personal guilt brings us into contact with him and makes it possible for us to be cleansed from our sins by the blood of the crucified Christ. This, in turn, brings us into fellowship not only with God himself but with other believers as well.

Walking in God's Light (2:1-11). John explains that he is writing in order to prevent his readers from committing sin, but he notes, as a realist, that for those who have offended God, Jesus is both our expiation and our advocate before the Father. On the more positive side of this equation, John offers reassuring criteria that can help us determine whether God's love and truth are active within us. If we live as Jesus lived and follow his commandments, then we can say that we know him and that we are united with him.

The most essential and concrete expression of our obedience shows itself in our decision to act charitably toward one another. This commandment was already revealed in an elementary form in the Old Testament, but it is displayed in a new and more challenging form in the heroic charity that Jesus demonstrated. The question of love can be a useful gauge for anyone. After all, no matter what people claim, if they love, they are walking in the light; but if they do not, they are being blinded by a darkness that has taken the form of hatred.

Standing against the World (2:12-19). Eager to touch the hearts of all of his readers, John addresses three different groups: fathers, young men, and children. He reminds each group of their religious "attainments," and then immediately cautions them against letting a love of the "world" distract them from their commitment to fulfilling God's will.

At the time when he was writing, John saw the "world" most poignantly—and most threateningly—in a group that was once associated with his church but whom he now brands as "anti-christs." Without naming them individually or giving further details, he identifies the essence of their betrayal: they have severed themselves from the faith of those who accept Jesus as the Messiah. Moreover, their denial of Jesus' true relationship with the Father has revealed that their earlier claims of belonging to the community of faith were hypocritical lies.

Anointed, Protected Children of God (2:20–3:3). John's pastoral reaction to the desertions of these people is primarily a concern to defend those who "know the truth." He is afraid that the renegades might lure more sheep from the flock, and so he warns his people against being enticed by what may seem like "advanced" knowledge. Following such false teachings will only rob them of the protective "anointing" in the truth through which they were brought into a living relationship with the Lord. Only by persevering in this apostolic teaching can they safeguard the promise of eternal life.

John's call for his people to abide in Christ is based on a plea for loyal gratitude to God for having made them his sons and daughters—an unmerited gift freely given. This privilege is only the beginning of a relationship which, if they maintain it faithfully, guarantees protection at the second coming of the Christ. Amazingly, when that revelation occurs, "We shall be like him, for we shall see him as he is."

Deeds Must Complement Faith (3:4-18). John's forceful statements against sin, lawlessness, and the works of the devil imply that the apostates have been dismissing as optional or unimportant the standards of behavior that Jesus had taught. John is unwilling to tolerate any such rationalization. A correct grasp of Jesus and his mission had to be supported by an equally strong commitment to Jesus' demanding code of conduct.

"This is the message you have heard from the beginning." This mention of "the beginning" reminds John that the first reported violation of the command to love is found in the story of Cain's murder of his brother, Abel. If this struggle between the forces of light and darkness is so deeply rooted in human history, John reasons, then the disciples of the one who taught us to love by laying his life down can hardly be surprised when the world also persecutes them. Those who allow themselves to hate show that they are spiritually dead, while those who genuinely love possess an inner life that empowers them to imitate Jesus, even in his self-sacrifice.

Listen to Your Spirit-filled Conscience (3:19–4:6). For those seeking confirmation that they are thinking and acting in line with God's will, one dependable gauge is their own conscience. John is convinced that the Spirit can bring God's voice into this process of discernment. And because he is the Spirit of Christ, he can illuminate those who are honestly trying to align their thoughts and actions with the sincere religious convictions they have developed from their contact with the apostolic tradition.

The world and its false prophets will try to disrupt this work of the Spirit by sowing doubt and deceit. In such cases, we should cling to the conviction that Jesus Christ has come in the flesh and that he is one with the Father. By doing this, we are already counteracting the spirits of deceit, because faithfulness to the truth demonstrates a presence of God within us that is beyond their understanding. Their very refusal to accept what we profess only confirms that they belong to the world of the antichrists.

Imitating God's Love Conforms Us to Him and Frees Us from Fear (4:7–5:12). Right belief, then, must be brought to completion by responding to God's love—and in such a way that we transform *his* initiative into *our own* love for others. By embracing this imitation of Christ, we drive out fear from our hearts because it is as we reach out to others in love that we ultimately understand what being loved means. By the same token, a genuine love for the God we cannot see is possible only in those who learn about love by loving the human beings they can see.

Left to our own devices, we would not be able to withstand the world's attempts to corrupt us and confound us. But our faith in Jesus opens us to the Spirit's power and helps convince us of the power of Jesus' blood to cleanse our hearts. The Spirit, too, gives us confidence in the God who raised Jesus from the dead and who has made us his adopted children. Thus, we know that we can overcome the world through loving obedience to Jesus and through love for the other children of God. All of this—confidence, faith, trust, the Spirit's power—is proof that eternal life dwells within us.

Hold On to the Truth and Pray for the Wavering (5:13-21). The final verses of the epistle are a kind of postscript. Through repetition, they emphasize John's conviction that those who are committed to Jesus already possess eternal life, while those who have cut themselves off from their brothers and sisters in faith have committed a kind of spiritual suicide.

There is a third group, however, that consists of those who have faltered sinfully in their trust and obedience. These can still be rescued. Our privileged status as adopted brothers and sisters of Jesus brings with it the responsibility to intercede for these brothers and sisters. But take care! Our own recognition of the truth, and our ability to choose the one who is truth itself, are gifts that must be carefully protected from any counterfeit belief.

WALKING IN THE LIGHT OF TRUTH

1 John 1:1-4

[1] We declare to you what was from the beginning, what we have heard, what we have seen with our eyes, what we have looked at and touched with our hands, concerning the word of life—[2]this life was revealed, and we have seen it and testify to it, and declare to you the eternal life that was with the Father and was revealed to us—[3]we declare to you what we have seen and heard so that you also may have fellowship with us; and truly our fellowship is with the Father and with his Son Jesus Christ. [4]We are writing these things so that our joy may be complete. ⚘

As he began his first letter, St. John beautifully expressed the reality of his experience of Jesus. As the eternal Son of God, Jesus existed from the very beginning, but he entered space and time as a man, and John was blessed to have seen and heard and touched him. But the key to John's blessing is not so much that he experienced the physical presence of Jesus. After all, thousands of people in first-century Israel encountered Jesus. What was so important for John is that he also came to an experience of Jesus as the Word of life, the one who gives divine life to all who believe.

John is a testimony to the fact that the gospel is meant to be *experienced*, that Jesus is meant to be experienced as the living God. The promise of the gospel is that we too can know Jesus as intimately as John did. Jesus is not bound by the laws of space and time. Because he has sent the Holy Spirit—God himself—to dwell in our hearts, we can all be filled with the presence of Jesus. We can hear his voice, know his love, and be changed by his grace.

This is why Jesus became man in the first place. God became human so that men and women could experience the presence and power of God. Let's not diminish the power of this good news!

John knew Jesus as he came in the flesh and walked among the people of his time; but more important, he also knew the Lord Jesus after his resurrection. It is the *risen* Lord that we can know! He is real and alive to us today. Do you want to truly know Jesus? Ask the Holy Spirit to reveal him to you. Ask him for an "empty-tomb" experience, for the knowledge deep in your heart that Jesus loves you unconditionally and that he has rescued you from sin and death. Jesus wants to come to you with more of his power and presence than you have known. Ask, and you will receive.

"Holy Spirit, open my eyes and heart to see Jesus more fully. Help me to experience Jesus, living and present within me. Help me to know him deep in my heart."

1 John 1:5–2:2

⁵ This is the message we have heard from him and proclaim to you, that God is light and in him there is no darkness at all. ⁶If we say that we have fellowship with him while we are walking in darkness, we lie and do not do what is true; ⁷but if we walk in the light as he himself is in the light, we have fellowship with one another, and the blood of Jesus his Son cleanses us from all sin. ⁸If we say that we have no sin, we deceive ourselves, and the truth is not in us. ⁹If we confess our sins, he who is faithful and just will forgive us our sins and cleanse us from all unrighteousness. ¹⁰If we say that we have not sinned, we make him a liar, and his word is not in us. ²ⁱ My little children, I am writing these things to you so that you may not sin. But if anyone does sin, we have an advocate with the Father, Jesus Christ the righteous; ²and he is the atoning sacrifice for our sins, and not for ours only but also for the sins of the whole world. ⌖

L ight, darkness, sin, forgiveness. John dives into these four powerful themes immediately after his short prologue. Let's unpack them a bit here, looking especially at how John uses them to offer his readers—and us—a measure of God's consolation and comfort.

"God is light and in him there is no darkness at all" (1 John 1:5). John uses the concept of light as a metaphor for truth and goodness, for all that is right and good in the world—just as any other moralistic writer of his time would do. But John goes one step further than other writers when he says that *God* is truth and goodness.

This "light" that is God is contrasted with the "darkness" that is inherent in all falsehood, evil, and deception. And because of its very nature, darkness cannot exist in God. So right from the start, John is telling us that the one to whom we have given our lives is worthy of our trust and confidence. He will never deceive us or be false to us. He will always give us what is true and good.

Next, we meet the theme of sin. It seems that some members of John's church had been denying sin or were saying that since Jesus has risen, sin is now obsolete and powerless. But John affirms that sin is still real—and is still a real threat. He goes on to promise, however, that by acknowledging not only the reality of sin but also our own sinfulness, we take the first steps in getting free from its hold. There's nothing like honest repentance to deprive sin and darkness of their power, and John is quick to sound that theme.

Finally, John comes to his last main theme: the forgiveness of our sins. Not only can we be set free from the power of sin; every sin we have ever committed (or ever will commit) can be washed away, just as if it had never happened. John understood that this is why Jesus had shed his blood: to cleanse us and release us from a guilty conscience (1 John 3:19-22).

What good news all of this is! What consolation it brings! But more than providing consolation, these truths can also provide a starting point for us to share the gospel with others. So as you read through this powerful letter from John, ask God to deepen your understanding of these four central truths, and then go out and use them as you let the light of Christ in you dispel the darkness around you.

"Father, thank you for sending your Son, Jesus Christ. Deepen in me these four themes of light, darkness, sin, and forgiveness, that I might effectively share your light and life with others."

1 John 2:3-11

3 Now by this we may be sure that we know him, if we obey his commandments. ⁴Whoever says, "I have come to know him," but does not obey his commandments, is a liar, and in such a person the truth does not exist; ⁵but whoever obeys his word, truly in this person the love of God has reached perfection. By this we may be sure that we are in him: ⁶whoever says, "I abide in him," ought to walk just as he walked.

7 Beloved, I am writing you no new commandment, but an old commandment that you have had from the beginning; the old commandment is the word that you have heard. ⁸Yet I am writing you a new commandment that is true in him and in you, because the darkness is passing away and the true light is already shining. ⁹Whoever says, "I am in the light," while hating a brother or sister, is still in the darkness. ¹⁰Whoever loves a brother or sister lives in the light, and in such a person there is no cause for stumbling. ¹¹But whoever hates another believer is in the darkness, walks in the darkness, and does not know the way to go, because the darkness has brought on blindness. ☙

Whoever loves a brother or a sister lives in the light. (1 John 2:10)

J esus wants our love for one another to be the clearest, most powerful sign to the world of the love of God and the validity of the gospel. As the saying goes, "You may be the only Bible another person will ever read." When discussing methodology for spreading the kingdom of God, all the words in the world pale in comparison to the Christlike witness of true love. Why? Because even though sin has the power to separate and isolate, the witness of healing and reconciliation between people shows the even greater power of God.

Jesus told us, "Love one another as I have loved you" (John 15:12). Can you imagine how different our families and workplaces would be if each of us loved the way Jesus loved? If we put to death all anger, greed, slander, bitterness, gossip, and jealousy, what a peaceful world we would have! St. John tells us that anyone who claims to abide in Jesus "ought to walk just as he walked" (1 John 2:6). We dream of preaching the gospel or performing miracles the way Jesus did. But what about loving the way Jesus did?

Sometimes people hurt us. People may even intentionally cause us pain. We may feel justified in responding with anger and resentment. But how did Jesus treat his persecutors? He forgave them and prayed for them (Luke 23:33-34). With an intense, unconditional love he sought to lead them into the kingdom. In a similar way, prodigal sons and daughters will not return to the Father's house until that house is filled with the Father's love.

Is there someone in your life whom you find very difficult to love? Forgetting what *they* should do, how will *you* be a minister of reconciliation? How will *you* love them into the kingdom? It won't be easy. It may not happen overnight. But remember: you have the Holy Spirit living in you, and in him all things are possible. Remember too that the fruit of reconciliation and mutual love is worth all the dying to ourselves that it takes to get there.

"Lord Jesus, fill my heart to overflowing with your love. Grant me the grace I need to seek reconciliation with my family, friends, and co-workers. Thank you for your goodness to me!"

1 John 2:12-17

12 I am writing to you, little children,
   because your sins are forgiven on account of his name.
13 I am writing to you, fathers,
   because you know him who is from the beginning.
I am writing to you, young people,
   because you have conquered the evil one.
14 I write to you, children,
   because you know the Father.
I write to you, fathers,
   because you know him who is from the beginning.
I write to you, young people,
   because you are strong
   and the word of God abides in you,
      and you have overcome the evil one.
15 Do not love the world or the things in the world. The love of the Father is not in those who love the world; 16for all that is in the world—the desire of the flesh, the desire of the eyes, the pride in riches—comes not from the Father but from the world. 17And the world and its desire are passing away, but those who do the will of God live forever.

What is the difference between having our hearts set on the world and having our hearts set on Jesus (1 John 2:15)? To answer that question, we must first understand what John meant by "the world." He wasn't speaking of the created order, which is still very good (Genesis 1:31). Nor was he saying that everything in society is hopelessly sinful. Rather, he was speaking of a mindset focused only on the finite world. For John, "the world" means a way of thinking that forgets about God and puts itself first.

John wrote that, while this worldly way of life may appear attractive for a time, it is ultimately unsatisfying, fruitless, and fleeting. This is in stark contrast to the way of life of those who love God. However old they may be, they are young and vigorous (1 John 2:12-14)! They have experienced forgiveness of their sins. Their hearts are capable of experiencing and understanding heavenly realities. They have a personal relationship with Jesus. They are forward-looking visionaries who are learning to see their lives and the world around them from a heavenly perspective. With joy and purpose, they dedicate themselves to advancing the kingdom of God on earth even as they go about their everyday lives.

Christianity is not meant to turn us into dreamers filled with naïve idealism. Rather, it makes us realists who see the darkness in the world but are filled with confidence in the power of Christ to overcome the darkness and establish God's kingdom.

This is the life in store for anyone who sets out to follow Jesus. Does it sound too good to be true? Does it seem too hard? Are we still too attracted to the things of "this world"? Each of us can come to know the vitality of the Christian life. It is not based on our personalities, but on the transforming power of the Holy Spirit in us. It is the result of having a living friendship with Jesus.

"Dear Jesus, I am far from perfect, but I want to live as St. John described. I give myself to you and ask you to fill me with your Holy Spirit. Enable me to love you and serve you!"

1 John 2:18-21

¹⁸ Children, it is the last hour! As you have heard that antichrist is coming, so now many antichrists have come. From this we know that it is the last hour. ¹⁹They went out from us, but they did not belong to us; for if they had belonged to us, they would have remained with us. But by going out they made it plain that none of them belongs to us. ²⁰But you have been anointed by the Holy One, and all of you have knowledge. ²¹I write to you, not because you do not know the truth, but because you know it, and you know that no lie comes from the truth.

But you have been anointed by the Holy One. (1 John 2:20)

Have you ever thought of yourself as having been "anointed" by God? In ancient Semitic culture, oil was a valued commodity. It penetrated deeply into the body and was believed to bring strength, health, and refreshment. The sick were anointed with oil. To pour oil on a guest was a sign of honor. Kings were anointed by priests to show that they had been chosen by God as his servants.

When we were baptized, we were anointed with sacred chrism—perfumed oil consecrated by the bishop. Chrism "signifies the gift of the Holy Spirit to the newly baptized, who has become a Christian, that is, one 'anointed' by the Holy Spirit, incorporated into Christ who is anointed priest, prophet and king" (*Catechism of the Catholic Church*, 1241).

As we go about our daily lives, we may not always *feel* anointed. We can be confused by what the world offers as wisdom. We can be uncertain about what the Lord wants us to do with our lives. We can be hesitant to tell others about Christ.

Yet, our anointing means that we have been brought into an intimate relationship with Jesus. As we draw closer to the Lord, we can fully expect our "heart knowledge" of God to grow. Through a committed prayer life, we have the opportunity to know the love of Jesus more deeply and to better understand the spiritual truths and realities of our faith. Every day, we should take the time to sit quietly before the Lord and listen to him. We need to ask God to help us recall his promises to us. Through our anointing we become God's "chosen race, a royal priesthood, a holy nation, God's own people" (1 Peter 2:9). Someday, by God's grace and mercy, we will sit beside our Lord at the heavenly banquet table. For now, we can use the gifts God has given us to build up the body of Christ on earth and bring others to the table as well.

"Lord, we offer ourselves to you. Keep us ever open to your love and mercy, and through your anointing, give us the grace to become more faithful disciples. Keep within us the hope and knowledge that someday we will see you face to face. Amen."

1 John 2:22-28

²²Who is the liar but the one who denies that Jesus is the Christ? This is the antichrist, the one who denies the Father and the Son. ²³No one who denies the Son has the Father; everyone who confesses the Son has the Father also. ²⁴Let what you heard from the beginning abide in you. If what you heard from the beginning abides in you, then you will abide in the Son and in the Father. ²⁵And this is what he has promised us, eternal life.
²⁶ I write these things to you concerning those who would deceive you. ²⁷As for you, the anointing that you received from him abides in you, and so you do not need anyone to teach you. But as his

anointing teaches you about all things, and is true and is not a lie, and just as it has taught you, abide in him.

[28] And now, little children, abide in him, so that when he is revealed we may have confidence and not be put to shame before him at his coming. ✑

Sometimes we can wind up feeling empty. Events can leave us doubting our faith and the decisions it has led us to make. The writer of 1 John addressed just that issue in his community. The community had undergone a painful split, and some who had remained faithful to the gospel as they knew it were second-guessing their decision. John wrote this letter to encourage them and help them deal with their confusion.

John proclaims that "everyone who confesses the Son has the Father also" (1 John 2:23). Do we believe in Christ? Have we embraced his salvation, which is ours by faith? Jesus' light has overcome the darkness in our hearts to bring us to the Father, spotless and clean. All he asks is that we invite him into our hearts. Every day, we can take a small step of faith simply by saying, "I believe in Jesus." The more we profess this simple truth, the more the Holy Spirit will open us to receive Jesus' salvation.

Jesus' anointing abides in us and teaches us everything (1 John 2:27). The power of his coming is complete; it needs only our embrace. The victory he has won for us is available to us immediately and comprehensively. Jesus has placed his love in our hearts and given us the Spirit of wisdom to teach us all things. Through the Spirit, we have all that we need to embrace the Father's love. Repentance, confession, and turning to Christ bring immediate victory and, ultimately, eternal life.

We can turn to Jesus at *any* time during the day. This is our right as God's children. No one can take it from us. Let us not be robbed of our inheritance of Jesus' presence in our lives. We can cry out to God; his anointing surrounds us and resides in us. Jesus has shared in our nature completely and knows all our struggles. When we were sinners, he died for us. And, now risen in glory, "he has remembered his steadfast love and faithfulness" (Psalm 98:3).

"Father, through Jesus, you have made a way for us to come to you. In baptism, we received your anointing, and that gift will be ours forever. Help us open our hearts to your Spirit, that we may see miracles in our lives."

1 John 2:29–3:6

29 If you know that he is righteous, you may be sure that everyone who does right has been born of him.
3:1 See what love the Father has given us, that we should be called children of God; and that is what we are. The reason the world does not know us is that it did not know him. 2Beloved, we are God's children now; what we will be has not yet been revealed. What we do know is this: when he is revealed, we will be like him, for we will see him as he is. 3And all who have this hope in him purify themselves, just as he is pure.
4 Everyone who commits sin is guilty of lawlessness; sin is lawlessness. 5You know that he was revealed to take away sins, and in him there is no sin. 6No one who abides in him sins; no one who sins has either seen him or known him. ✐

And all who have this hope in him purify themselves, just as he is pure.
(1 John 3:3)

Our hope is in the Lord. And God, whose promises never fail, will surely give us all we can hope for in him. The Greek word for hope, *elpo*, means to anticipate, to expect, to place confidence in. Theses are not words of *possibility*. These are words of *certainty*. When we place our hope in the Lord, we can be certain that he will not fail us. God is trustworthy and faithful—he will bring about his promises. For our part, he asks that we believe and trust in him.

Our hope is that one day we will be so filled with the life and love of our God that we will actually become like Jesus (1 John 3:2). On that day, we will be presented to God—holy, free of reproach and blame (Colossians 1:22). Our response while we eagerly await this fulfillment is to treasure these promises and obey God's word. His promises are true and will come about. Our Father has fulfilled his perfect plan through Jesus, our Savior.

We can believe in God's promises, even when our sin or difficult situations discourage us. It is true, we may not see immediate results: we will still see sin, and we will always want to see more change. None of us is perfect. Still, we can place our hope in God, who is true to his word. By the power of his Spirit, Jesus has enabled us to become perfect, as he and the Father are perfect.

Let us place our hope in Jesus. Anything else will fall short of the fullness of life that God wants to give us. As we learn to rely on him and his great promises, our lives will change. We will be confident and secure in our God. He will never disappoint us, never let us down. Instead, he will enable us to face our sin and weaknesses with hope, knowing that Jesus has won our full redemption.

"Holy Spirit, awaken our hope in Jesus, our cornerstone. He has won a place for us with the Father and is ever at work in us. Help us to believe in the promises of God, and to proclaim them to others."

1 John 3:7-10

[7]Little children, let no one deceive you. Everyone who does what is right is righteous, just as he is righteous. [8]Everyone who commits sin is a child of the devil; for the devil has been sinning from the beginning. The Son of God was revealed for this purpose, to destroy the works of the devil. [9]Those who have been born of God do not sin, because God's seed abides in them; they cannot sin, because they have been born of God. [10]The children of God and the children of the devil are revealed in this way: all who do not do what is right are not from God, nor are those who do not love their brothers and sisters. ✌

The Son of God was revealed for this purpose, to destroy the works of the devil. (1 John 3:8)

Scripture is clear that there is a real devil who seeks the ruin of souls. He seeks death over life and bondage over freedom. Cunning and deceitful, he is a master at sowing seeds of despair and mistrust. The good news is, however, that God our Father sent Jesus to destroy the works of Satan so that we can embrace eternal life. That's a pretty tall order! In fact, it's so immense a claim that we can sometimes overlook the implications for our day-to-day lives.

We often think about the "works of the devil" only in terms of blatant temptations and unspeakable sins. But Satan is very cunning. Chief among his "works" are subtle lies about God's character; accusations that keep us mired in guilt; quietly whispered words of division and mistrust against family members, friends, and even enemies; and a constant harping on our weaknesses that robs us of hope.

As threatening as all this sounds, we can still have great confidence. Why? Because all of Satan's ploys have been overpowered by

135

the cross of Christ. Nothing need become an insurmountable obstacle to someone giving his or her life to Jesus. If we want to evangelize effectively, we must be alert to the devil's ploys in those with whom we are seeking to share the gospel. Satan will try any tactic to keep people from opening their hearts to Jesus. He will even try to convince us that evangelism is just too hard for us, or that it's just not our calling. Nothing could be further from the truth.

Let us pray for God's protection over ourselves and those to whom we minister. Let us take our stand against the devil's schemes and ask Jesus to soften the hearts of unbelievers. Whenever you detect his strategies, don't worry or give up. The infant in the manger is a warrior in the heavens! He has conquered all! Let us be aware of who we are in Jesus and the freedom he has won for us—a freedom available to everyone if they reach out to him in trust.

"Lord Jesus, we praise you and love you. Thank you for overcoming the devil by the love of God. Appear in us and others that all might live with you forever."

1 John 3:11-22

[11] For this is the message you have heard from the beginning, that we should love one another. [12]We must not be like Cain who was from the evil one and murdered his brother. And why did he murder him? Because his own deeds were evil and his brother's righteous. [13]Do not be astonished, brothers and sisters, that the world hates you. [14]We know that we have passed from death to life because we love one another. Whoever does not love abides in death. [15]All who hate a brother or sister are murderers, and you know that murderers do not have eternal life abiding in them. [16]We know love by this, that he laid down his life for us—and we ought to lay down our lives

for one another. [17]How does God's love abide in anyone who has the world's goods and sees a brother or sister in need and yet refuses help?

[18] Little children, let us love, not in word or speech, but in truth and action. [19]And by this we will know that we are from the truth and will reassure our hearts before him [20]whenever our hearts condemn us; for God is greater than our hearts, and he knows everything. [21]Beloved, if our hearts do not condemn us, we have boldness before God; [22]and we receive from him whatever we ask, because we obey his commandments and do what pleases him. ✍

John provided a standard by which we may determine if we have truly "passed from death to life" (1 John 3:14). The standard is love for one another. Indeed, we are called to go beyond that and love even those who hate us (see Matthew 5:44). The love that is required is a love that expresses itself in deeds, not just in words or sentiment.

The deeds of love can be large or small; John spoke of both laying down one's life and giving alms to the poor as examples of love. But whether large or small, the actions must be performed, not merely talked about or endorsed in theory. Those who do not love by their actions are those who abide in death. Conversely, if we do express our love through our deeds, we can "reassure our hearts" that we are "from the truth" (1 John 3:19).

St. Augustine (354–430) addressed this kind of love in one of his homilies. Perfect love, he told his hearers, is expressed in laying down our lives; but if we don't feel that we yet have this perfect love, we shouldn't let that stop us from finding actions to express the love that we already do possess.

One action that is within nearly everyone's reach, according to Augustine, is the giving of alms. It is an excellent place to start, he reasoned, because if you are unable to provide for your brother's needs, you could never expect to manage to give your life for him: "If you are not yet equal to the dying for your brother, be even now equal to the giving of your means to your brother. . . . If in your abundance you cannot give to your brother, can you lay down your life for your brother? . . . He is your brother, alike you are bought; one is the price paid for you; you are both redeemed by the blood of Christ. See whether you have mercy, if you have this world's means" (Homily on 1 John, 5.12).

We can pray that this virtue of love expressed in deeds will be increased in our lives, to the benefit of God's people throughout the world.

"Lord, teach us to look for ways to love others, both at home and in other lands. Teach us to be generous with our worldly possessions, for we are one family, caring for one another's needs."

1 John 3:23–4:6

[21]Beloved, if our hearts do not condemn us, we have boldness before God; [22]and we receive from him whatever we ask, because we obey his commandments and do what pleases him.

[23] And this is his commandment, that we should believe in the name of his Son Jesus Christ and love one another, just as he has commanded us. [24]All who obey his commandments abide in him, and he abides in them. And by this we know that he abides in us, by the Spirit that he has given us.

[4:1] Beloved, do not believe every spirit, but test the spirits to see whether they are from God; for many false prophets have gone out into the world. [2]By this you know the Spirit of God: every spirit that confesses that Jesus Christ has come in the flesh is from God, [3]and every spirit that does not confess Jesus is not from God. And this is the spirit of the antichrist, of which you have heard that it is coming; and now it is already in the world. ⁴Little children, you are from God, and have conquered them; for the one who is in you is greater than the one who is in the world. ⁵They are from the world; therefore what they say is from the world, and the world listens to them. ⁶We are from God. Whoever knows God listens to us, and whoever is not from God does not listen to us. From this we know the spirit of truth and the spirit of error. 🜚

This is his commandment, that we should believe in the name of his Son.
(1 John 3:23)

Why would St. John tell us we should believe in the name of Jesus? Because John understood that a person's name represents everything that person is. So Jesus' name—which means "the Lord saves"—represents Jesus' integrity, honor, and character. As Christians, we are called to do everything in the name of Jesus (Colossians 3:17). We gather in his name; we give thanks to God in his name; we are to live in a way that glorifies his name.

At Jesus' baptism, a voice from heaven declared, "This is my Son, the Beloved, with whom I am well pleased" (Matthew 3:17). Later in his ministry, Jesus appealed to the Father to glorify his name, and in reply the Father declared that he would (John 12:28). St. Paul tells us that ultimately every knee must bend at the name of Jesus (Philippians 2:9-11). There is power in the name of Jesus, because the Father has exalted Jesus above all others, and his name above all other names. The apostles believed so strongly in this that they performed many healings and miracles using the name of Jesus.

Let's be careful with this. We're not meant to use the name of

Jesus as if it were a magic word. God wants us to believe in the person being named: Jesus Christ. To believe in his name is to believe that Jesus can heal the sick, deliver us from evil, and open the gates to the kingdom of God. It is also to believe that Jesus is merciful, just, kind, and loving; that he is seated at the right hand of God, where he intercedes for us day and night. This is our king whom we follow. This is our brother and friend, who loves us and is with us for all time!

"Jesus, I give you all praise and honor and glory forever. You are my Lord, who cares for me and guides me so that I may not go astray. I want to stand and live each day under the power and authority of your name."

1 John 4:7-10

7   Beloved, let us love one another, because love is from God; everyone who loves is born of God and knows God. 8Whoever does not love does not know God, for God is love. 9God's love was revealed among us in this way: God sent his only Son into the world so that we might live through him. 10In this is love, not that we loved God but that he loved us and sent his Son to be the atoning sacrifice for our sins.

It was out of his abundant love that God created us, and he promised that he will never stop loving us. Each day, he calls us to reflect his character by loving one another. But in trying to obey his call, we come face to face with our own inability to love. Our only hope is to allow Jesus' love *for us* to work *through us* as we reach out to others. God's love can fill us with the power to love far beyond our human limitations. What a joy it is to know what his love can accomplish through us!

Corrie ten Boom, who lived in Holland during World War II, was a powerful witness to the wonder of God's love. Corrie felt compelled by the love of God to hide persecuted Jews in her home until they could be transported safely out of the country. After having rescued hundreds of Jews, she was approached by a man requesting money to help his wife escape. Corrie, her family, and her friends scraped together what they could, only to have this man betray them. The Nazis arrested them all and sent them to a concentration camp, where eventually everyone except Corrie died.

Upon her release, Corrie became a popular preacher. After speaking at one rather large gathering, she was confronted by the man who had betrayed her. At first, hatred filled her heart, but as she turned to Jesus, she found herself filled with an inexplicable love for this man! Not only did she know peace, but she was able to forgive the very man who caused the deaths of her loved ones.

Eventually, Corrie wrote to this man and told him that she had forgiven him because of Jesus' love. The man replied that if Jesus could enable his followers to love to the point of such forgiveness, then there must be hope, even for him. That day, he gave his life to Jesus. In awe, Corrie later wrote, "God chose me, who had hated this man, to bring him to Jesus!"

We may never find ourselves called to love in the way that Corrie was called, but we all have opportunities to overcome mistrust, prejudice, and even hatred with Jesus' love. Who knows what Jesus' love, working through us, will accomplish!

"Lord Jesus, our own love is weak, and our hearts are small. But you have loved us first and given your life for us. Widen our hearts and let your love fill us to overflowing. We want to show the world what your love can do!"

1 John 4:11-14

¹¹Beloved, since God loved us so much, we also ought to love one another. ¹²No one has ever seen God; if we love one another, God lives in us, and his love is perfected in us.
¹³ By this we know that we abide in him and he in us, because he has given us of his Spirit. ¹⁴And we have seen and do testify that the Father has sent his Son as the Savior of the world. ¹⁵God abides in those who confess that Jesus is the Son of God, and they abide in God. ¹⁶So we have known and believe the love that God has for us.

God is love, and those who abide in love abide in God, and God abides in them. ¹⁷Love has been perfected among us in this: that we may have boldness on the day of judgment, because as he is, so are we in this world. ¹⁸There is no fear in love, but perfect love casts out fear; for fear has to do with punishment, and whoever fears has not reached perfection in love.

Since God loved us so much, we also ought to love one another.
(1 John 4:11)

Take some time today to ponder the love of God. He created you out of love, and it was because of his love that he sent his Son to die for your sins. Scripture characterizes God's love as warm and tender (Hosea 11:8), a combination of a father's care and encouragement (Psalm 103:13) and a mother's all-embracing comfort (Isaiah 66:13). God's love is also passionate and joyful: just as a groom rejoices over his bride, so God rejoices in us (Isaiah 62:5). His love is not based on anything good we have done, but on his nature, which is love (1 John 4:16).

Allow these truths to penetrate your heart and mind. Allow the love of God to soften your heart. As you do, you will find a new ability to love other people. God's love in you will overflow to others, even to those who do not love you, even to those who have hurt you. This is the nature of divine love—the love that Jesus demonstrated on the cross.

Your trust and reliance on God's love will also give you a confidence that you are safe from God's judgment (1 John 4:17-18). When your faith is in Jesus Christ and his atoning sacrifice, you will have nothing to fear from God. Putting aside fear, you can grow in love for God and focus your attention on pleasing him. No matter what your circumstances may be, you can lead a life free of fear and useless anxiety because your heavenly Father has you in the palms of his hands (Isaiah 49:16).

Today and every day, seek to know God's love more deeply. God loves to make himself present to you as you pray, study his word, and participate in the life of the church. As you do these things, allow God's love to refresh you so that you will have the strength to give of yourself to others. Cry out to the Lord with all your heart, and you will hear him speak to you deep within your spirit, "Take heart; it is I; do not be afraid" (Mark 6:50).

"Thank you, Holy Spirit, for pouring the love of God into my heart. I know that it is the same love with which the Father has always loved his Son. Help me to express your love to the people around me today."

1 John 4:19–5:4

[19]We love because he first loved us. [20]Those who say, "I love God," and hate their brothers or sisters, are liars; for those who do not love a brother or sister whom they have seen, cannot love God whom they have not seen. [21]The commandment we have from him is this:

WALKING IN THE LIGHT OF TRUTH

those who love God must love their brothers and sisters also.

⁵ᐟ¹ Everyone who believes that Jesus is the Christ has been born of God, and everyone who loves the parent loves the child. ²By this we know that we love the children of God, when we love God and obey his commandments. ³For the love of God is this, that we obey his commandments. And his commandments are not burdensome, ⁴for whatever is born of God conquers the world. And this is the victory that conquers the world, our faith. ☙

When Japan bombed Pearl Harbor in 1941, the United States had no choice but to enter the Second World War. Before then, politicians, army generals, and everyday citizens were locked in debates and arguments over whether to get involved. However, once the enemy struck them at home, the issue was resolved. The internal fighting and bickering ended. Troops were called up. Women entered the workforce as never before. Fuel, paper, and metal were rationed. Everything was directed toward victory.

Just as our country needed to mobilize its forces to win a victory in World War II, we need to mobilize ourselves to win a spiritual victory today. The enemy is already "on our soil"; in fact, it's inside every one of us. And that enemy, as you know, is sin.

Granted, our personal victory over sin would never make the evening news. But just imagine how different the world would be if everyone turned away from sin!

The good news is that God offers us victory, and the way to victory is surprisingly simple: we need to believe in Jesus. "The victory that conquers the world" is "our faith" (1 John 5:4). Do you want to overcome sin? Do you want to be free from the faults that trip you up every time? Do you want to be able to love that difficult neighbor, co-worker, or relative? Well, how's your faith?

To believe in Jesus means coming to a different way of understanding God, the world, and ourselves. Take a moment to consider which mental inputs will shape your thinking today. Will you watch an extra hour of television, or take time to read Scripture? When you have a spare moment, will you daydream, or will you turn to Jesus? Will you allow your mind to teem with anxieties, or will you make an act of trust in God's care for you?

If you spend time with Jesus, the results may surprise you. As your mind fills with truth, you will become alert to the Holy Spirit, and to the battle between spirit and flesh—and you will be better able to follow the Spirit. In short, your heart will be changed as your mind is transformed (Romans 12:2). Then, victory will be yours.

"Lord Jesus, fill my mind and transform me. I adore you, for you are the truth that will lead me away from sin."

1 John 5:5-13

⁵Who is it that conquers the world but the one who believes that Jesus is the Son of God?

⁶ This is the one who came by water and blood, Jesus Christ, not with the water only but with the water and the blood. And the Spirit is the one that testifies, for the Spirit is the truth. ⁷There are three that testify: ⁸the Spirit and the water and the blood, and these three agree. ⁹If we receive human testimony, the testimony of God is greater; for this is the testimony of God that he has testified to his Son. ¹⁰Those who believe in the Son of God have the testimony in their hearts. Those who do not believe in God have made him a liar by not believing in the testimony that God has given concerning his Son. ¹¹And this is the testimony: God gave us eternal life, and this life is in his Son. ¹²Whoever has the Son has life; whoever does not have the Son of God does not have life.

¹³ I write these things to you who believe in the name of the Son of God, so that you may know that you have eternal life. ✎

Faith can baffle the mind. In our efforts to understand it intellectually, we run the risk of missing it completely. Yet, when the Holy Spirit gives us faith—or increases our faith—as a generous gift, our lives can be radically changed. The key is *receiving* the grace and blessings of God by faith and allowing that grace to change our lives. Study and intellectual understanding are important, and we should pursue them. But they can never replace the Spirit's work in us.

The author of 1 John wrote to a community that had undergone a painful division (1 John 2:18-19). Anyone who has witnessed, or even experienced, the pain of a divorce can understand how devastating the breakdown of close relationships can be. Nothing can hurt as deeply as a sense of betrayed trust. Responding to his community's division, the author sought to keep his people's eyes fixed on the Lord, who would help them through a difficult time.

In his letter, the author tried to bring his readers back to the most basic of truths: believe that Jesus is the Son of God (1 John 5:5). He encouraged them not just to accept this truth intellectually, but to trust it based on the testimonies that they had heard and that had built faith in them. He warned them not to look at the call to believe as merely accepting a set of propositions. Faith is a relationship that grows over time as we come to experience God's love and place our trust in him.

We have many wonderful testimonies to the gospel. However, simply accepting them intellectually will not give us the power and joy that God so wants us to have. Without a living faith, we will never be able to overcome sin or to experience the depths of God's love. The testimonies that exist—the water of baptism; Jesus' blood in the Eucharist; and the Spirit leading us to Christ—all work together to bring faith alive in us. Let us open our hearts to God, trusting that he will fill us more and more. We can never get enough of the Holy Spirit.

"Holy Spirit, we believe. Help our unbelief. Help us to trust in you fully. Lead us today. Speak to us. Comfort us. Above all, help us to love Jesus so much that we fully trust him."

1 John 5:14-21

[14] And this is the boldness we have in him, that if we ask anything according to his will, he hears us. [15]And if we know that he hears us in whatever we ask, we know that we have obtained the requests made of him. [16]If you see your brother or sister committing what is not a mortal sin, you will ask, and God will give life to such a one—to those whose sin is not mortal. There is sin that is mortal; I do not say that you should pray about that. [17]All wrongdoing is sin, but there is sin that is not mortal.

[18] We know that those who are born of God do not sin, but the one who was born of God protects them, and the evil one does not touch them. [19]We know that we are God's children, and that the whole world lies under the power of the evil one. [20]And we know that the Son of God has come and has given us understanding so that we may know him who is true; and we are in him who is true, in his Son Jesus Christ. He is the true God and eternal life.

[21] Little children, keep yourselves from idols.

God will hear us! This is the staggering promise made to all who believe in Jesus: "If we ask anything according to his will he hears us" (1 John 5:14). Does it seem incredible that the creator of the whole universe, the one whom wind and waves obey, could truly be attuned to our individual requests? Yet it is amazingly, wonderfully true! Our Father not only hears every prayer we make but delights in answering us.

God is all good, and he wants only what is eternally good for us. Do we feel that our prayers are going unanswered and wonder why God does not move more quickly? If so, we should consider the words of John the Baptist: "He must increase, but I must decrease" (John 3:30). The times when we feel very sure what God should do are the very times when we should decrease. Why? Because God is not only infinitely more loving than we are, he is also infinitely wiser than we are. We believe in him not because he constantly gives us what we want but because he has shown himself to be absolutely trustworthy. So let God increase in you. Let him decide what is truly best; let him shape your mind and heart to desire his will more than your own.

Take Jesus as your model. He "offered up prayers and supplications, with loud cries and tears, to the one who was able to save him from death, and he was heard because of his reverent submission. Although he was a Son, he learned obedience through what he suffered" (Hebrews 5:7-8). For us, as for Jesus, God's good plan may sometimes be different from what we prayed for. It may even involve pain. However, his plan is always to produce a greater good in us, in those around us, and in the world. As we decrease and let Jesus fill us, we will ultimately see the beauty and creativity of God's plan.

How can we grow in confidence that God hears and answers all of our prayers? If we put our lives in our heavenly Father's hands, he will strengthen our faith. God knows our deepest desires and will deepen our trust that he is working to bring all things to good in our lives.

"Heavenly Father, I place my trust in you and your plan for my life. Have your way in me."

Truth, Love, and the Challenges of Life in Community

The Second and Third Letters of John

Truth, Love, and the Challenges of Life in Community

An Introduction to the Second and Third Letters of John

Rev. Joseph F. Wimmer, OSA

Five works of the New Testament are attributed to "John": a gospel, the Book of Revelation, and three letters. According to popular Christian imagination, all of them were written by John the apostle, one of the twelve and the "disciple whom Jesus loved" (John 21:7). Early church tradition, however, was more discriminating. Eusebius, in his *Ecclesiastical History* written about A.D. 325, states that

> Of the writings of John, not only his Gospel but also the first of his epistles has been accepted without dispute both now and in ancient times. But the other two are disputed. In regard to the Apocalypse, the opinions of most men are still divided. (3.24)

Contemporary scholars, drawing on various historical and literary sources, still dispute the precise relationship of the letters of 1, 2, and 3 John to one another, but they are generally agreed that 2 John was written first, followed by 3 John, with 1 John coming last. No matter when they were written, however, all of these letters are rich in theology and provide us with insights into the primitive church's Christian understanding of the meaning and message of Jesus.

2 John has all the earmarks of being a real letter, sent by "the presbyter" to "a lady who is elect and to her children." The "elect lady," however, is probably not an individual but rather an eccle-

sial community, for verse 4 expresses joy at finding "some of your children walking in the path of truth," and the letter ends with a greeting from "the children of your elect sister." Since 2 and 3 John are written in the same style, we may suppose that it was written by the same person. 3 John mentions a previous letter written by the author to "the church" led by a certain Diotrephes (3 John 9); perhaps that church is the "elect lady" of letter 2.

The author of both letters is a *presbyteros*, commonly translated as "elder" or "presbyter," and of course both letters are attributed to John. Could this *presbyteros* be the apostle John? That seems unlikely. Eusebius writes that according to Papias, who was a friend of Polycarp and a disciple of John the apostle, the title *presbyteros* referred not to the apostles, the eyewitnesses of the ministry of Jesus, but rather to their followers, the next generation of church leaders. With regard to John the presbyter, Eusebius says explicitly that according to Papias there were two men named John: the apostle, and "the other John" whom Papias "distinctly calls a presbyter" (*EH* 3.39).

2 John

2 John is only one page long. It consists of a salutation (verses 1-3), the body of the letter with two major themes—concern for mutual love (verses 4-6) and a warning about deceitful teachers (verses 7-11)—and a closing promise of a visit along with a set of greetings (verses 12-13).

Salutation (verses 1-3). In traditional style, the presbyter, probably a disciple of the apostle John and leader of the Johannine community, writes to "the elect lady" with love in truth, along with others who "know" the truth, a "truth that abides in us and will be with us forever."

THE CHURCH MOVES OUT

Love and truth are two central concepts of the Gospel of John and of the Johannine community. For John, truth (in Greek *ale-theia*) refers to the profound reality of God, and of God's will as expressed in the teaching of Jesus and his invitation to faith and love. This is the truth that abides in us forever (verses 2). It is the very reality of God that never ends but resides within us in mutual knowledge and love. Truth is here far more profound than particular teachings; it supports and underlies them.

Of course, the teachings themselves are important for the community, for they help define it against "deceivers" and those "who do not abide in the teaching of Christ" (verses 7-9). But these teachings retain their power and their claim on us because they spring from the truth of who Christ is. Knowledge (Greek *gnosis*) of this truth entails both experience and fidelity, a personal relationship. This knowledge is not theoretical but impels us to action. We are called to "walk in the truth" (verse 4), to "do the truth" (1 John 1:6). And this is where "love" comes in.

Love, *agape*, is truth's companion, and like truth, it also expresses the reality of God ("God is love" 1 John 4:16) and God's initiative of communion and salvation in Jesus. If the presbyter loves the elect lady and her children "in truth," it is by way of fellowship in the one community of Christ. The salutation ends with a blessing, not only of grace and peace as in the early Pauline letters, but also with mercy (as in 1 and 2 Timothy), God's compassion and forgiveness in Jesus.

Concern for Mutual Love (verses 4-6). The presbyter repeats the famous dictum of John, "let us love one another," but calls it "not a new commandment but one that we have had from the beginning" (verse 5). By using the first person plural, "let *us* love," the presbyter includes himself in God's commandment. The origin of that commandment is here attributed to God the Father, and the "beginning" is probably the beginning of the formation of the Christian community by Jesus himself.

The call for mutual love that is at the heart of community prepares the ground for a later rejection of the "deceivers" who would disturb that love by new teachings. Though springing forth within the community, mutual love of itself has a centrifugal tendency, an outward movement that eventually becomes universal. The "new commandment" of John 13:34, to love one another "as I have loved you," helps to underscore that universality; Jesus excluded no one from his love—neither should we.

Warning about Deceitful Teachers (verses 7-11). The presbyter is worried about the disruption of unity by certain deceitful teachers who "do not acknowledge Jesus Christ as coming in the flesh" (verse 7). Apparently this is a reference to Docetism, a heresy in the early church that was unable to accept the union of the divine and human in the one person, Jesus Christ.

The Docetists made a sharp distinction between Christ, the divine Son of God, and the human Jesus of Nazareth, who died on the cross. They claimed that Christ the Son of God was united to Jesus only temporarily, "in appearance." They received their name from the Greek word *dokein*, "to seem, to appear to be." Thus when Jesus died on the cross, this only "appeared" to be one person both human and divine. At its heart, Docetism is a refusal to acknowledge the incarnation, the very possibility of the true union of the divine and human.

The presbyter was so concerned by this false teaching that he even called those who promoted it the "antichrist" (verse 7). The word *antichristos* is used only five times in the New Testament, once here and four times in 1 John. The Greek word *anti* can either mean "instead of" or "against." Here it seems to have the latter meaning, someone who is against Christ. The term is not yet identified with Satan, though that would happen in the early Christian literature after the New Testament period. As deceivers, such itinerant preachers were not to be received into Christian homes or even be greeted. The stakes—the unity of faith in the early Christian community—were too high for believers to have any sustained contact with them.

Concluding Greetings (verses 12-13). In closing, the presbyter promises to visit the community, "so that our joy may be full." In Jewish tradition, such fullness of joy was reserved for the coming of the Messiah. Its use here implies that the early Christian community saw itself as living in the final, messianic age. How important it was, therefore, to remain rooted in the teaching and abiding truth and love of Christ.

3 John

This letter has many similarities to 2 John, and was doubtlessly written by the same presbyter, concerning the same Christian community as previously (see 3 John 9). This time, however, the author doesn't address the community directly but a man named Gaius, to whom he explains the difficulties he has with the community's leader Diotrephes. Gaius is apparently not a member of that community. The presbyter thanks him for his hospitality, not only toward himself but also toward Christian missionaries whom he does not even know, and encourages him to continue his "share in the work of truth" (verse 8). In particular, he commends to him a man named Demetrius.

The letter begins with a salutation, which includes the name of the sender and the addressee (verses 1-2). The body of the letter consists in praise and encouragement of Gaius, the addressee (verses 3-8); a warning against Diotrephes, leader of the community (verses 9-11); and a recommendation for Demetrius (verse 12). The letter ends with the promise of a personal visit and the sending of greetings (verses 13-15).

Salutation (verses 1-2). Gaius is not mentioned elsewhere in the New Testament. The presbyter calls him "beloved," that is, a fellow Christian. By calling Gaius one of his "children," he seems to indicate that he was the one who baptized Gaius (verse 4). The hope that Gaius is in good health follows the typical form of a Hellenistic letter, and is the only example of such a comment in the New Testament.

Praise of Gaius (verses 3-8). Some members of Gaius' community had come to the presbyter and borne witness to his "walking the path of truth" (verse 3), which meant fidelity to Christ and his fellow Christians in word and deed. Gaius' care for itinerant preachers whom he did not know is especially praised, since these preachers did not typically accept lodging in gentile homes. The presbyter then encourages Gaius to continue to support them and thus share in their ministry, the "work of truth" (verse 8).

Warning against Diotrephes (verses 9-11). As leader of a community—and a person who is also at enmity with another community—Diotrephes is mentioned only here, but his situation must have been all too common in early Christianity. It seems he had ignored a letter written to his church by the presbyter (quite possibly 2 John), and had refused to see delegates from the presbyter—probably because he did not want to be criticized for his understanding of the gospel. The issue must have been a serious one—quite possibly the whole question of Docetism, which was at the center of 2 John—for Diotrephes even expelled those members from his church who did welcome the delegates.

Recommendation for Demetrius (verse 12). The Demetrius on whose behalf the presbyter bears testimony is mentioned only here in the New Testament, but he may be the same Demetrius who was made bishop (*episkopos*) of Philadelphia by John the apostle (*Constitution of the Holy Apostles* 7.46). How he fits in here is unclear. Perhaps he is the bearer of the letter (3 John) from the presbyter to Gaius.

Conclusion and Greetings (verses 13-15). Verses 13 and 14 are almost the same as the concluding verses of 2 John. Verse 15—"Peace be with you"—is a greeting common in both the Old and New Testaments (see, for example, Genesis 43:23; Judges 6:23; Daniel 10:19; John 20:21; 1 Peter 5:14). It promises or prays for the fullness of security and the satisfaction of all one's needs. Such peace can only come from God and is the fruit of walking in the truth—the same truth that this presbyter held so dear.

2 John 1-3

[1] The elder to the elect lady and her children, whom I love in the truth, and not only I but also all who know the truth, [2]because of the truth that abides in us and will be with us forever:

[3] Grace, mercy, and peace will be with us from God the Father and from Jesus Christ, the Father's Son, in truth and love. ⟡

In these opening verses, the "presbyter" who wrote this letter mentions the word "truth" four times! Why this stress on the truth, and what does it mean for the author and his community? Most likely, he means the truth about God's coming to us in the flesh as Jesus Christ. It is the truth about Jesus, who he was, who he is, and what he has done for us in his death and resurrection. This is at the heart of his concern for this local church because many who once belonged to that church had begun to deny Jesus. And to counter these preachers of false doctrine, John urges his people to guard and treasure the truth that had set them free.

Unfortunately, even today we see distortions of the truth about Jesus. From best-selling novels to humanistic presentations about Jesus in the media, to the influence of various cults and sects, false ideas and teachings about Jesus abound, and we must be wary of them.

The truth that we hold—the truth that is at the heart of the church—is precious indeed, because it is a source of great joy and consolation. What could be a better foundation for life in this world than to know that the Son of God has come to us as a man, both to show us how to live and to offer his life so that we could become like him!

How can we grow in love for and understanding of the truth about Jesus? First, we can read and study the Scriptures, and especially the gospels, which tell us all about Jesus. Perhaps we can join our parish's Bible study or attend Scripture conferences in our diocese.

Next must surely come the teachings of the church, especially as they are presented in the *Catechism of the Catholic Church*. And of course, there is nothing like open discussion about what we are reading with trusted friends and mentors who are farther along on the road to holiness than we are. In all of these ways and more we can come to know Jesus better and walk in this truth about him.

Why not decide today to do something concrete to help you grow in the truth about Jesus? Ask the Lord to help you in this. You can be sure that this is one prayer that he loves to answer!

"Lord Jesus, come into my mind and heart more each day. Help me to know you, Lord, and to walk in your truth daily. Help me also to share this truth with others."

2 John 4-11

4 I was overjoyed to find some of your children walking in the truth, just as we have been commanded by the Father. 5But now, dear lady, I ask you, not as though I were writing you a new commandment, but one we have had from the beginning, let us love one another. 6And this is love, that we walk according to his commandments; this is the commandment just as you have heard it from the beginning—you must walk in it. 7Many deceivers have gone out into the world, those who do not confess that Jesus Christ has come in the flesh; any such person is the deceiver and the antichrist! 8Be on your guard, so that you do not lose what we have worked for, but may receive a full reward. 9Everyone who does not abide in the teaching of Christ, but goes beyond it, does not have God; whoever abides in

the teaching has both the Father and the Son. [10]Do not receive into the house or welcome anyone who comes to you and does not bring this teaching; [11]for to welcome is to participate in the evil deeds of such a person.

Even though you make many prayers, I will not listen. (Isaiah 1:15)

"If only I had more time and energy! Then I could pray more, read more Scripture, volunteer more service, and catch up on my to-do list!" Does this sound like you? It seems that we never have enough energy, time, or resources to get ahead. And if we push and try hard, we usually end up exhausting ourselves.

John addresses these issues when he states that "everyone who does not abide in the teaching of Christ, but goes beyond it, does not have God" (2 John 9), and as a consequence, does not have the support of God's peace and grace. What is the "teaching of Christ"? Simply this: "that Jesus Christ has come in the flesh" (verse 7). So to abide in the teaching of Christ is to believe—and rest our hope in—the fact that the Son of God loved us enough to become one like us and to take all our suffering and anxieties with him to the cross.

Have you ever tried to fly a kite or sail a boat on a breezy day? Once you catch the wind, you can glide effortlessly. It's like that with our life in Christ. Jesus has taken our place, and we are now in him. With him we can move mountains! God wants us to learn how to abide in his teaching as we rest in the assurance of his love and mercy. He knows better than we do how much we need his help and grace and wisdom. It's the very reason why he became man in the first place.

By abiding in the teaching of Christ, we can allow his grace to change us into his likeness. His peace—a peace which "surpasses all understanding" (Philippians 4:7)—can fill our hearts and free us to love others as fully as he loves us.

St. Thérèse of Lisieux once said, "I feel that when I am charitable it is Jesus alone who acts in me; the more I am united to him the more do I love all my sisters." The greatest gift we possess is the love of God made man, and the greatest freedom we have is to share that love with others. We can never outmatch God, who became one of us simply because he loves us.

"Thank you, Jesus, for your abiding presence and for the joy I can experience as I abide in you."

2 John 12-13

12 Although I have much to write to you, I would rather not use paper and ink; instead I hope to come to you and talk with you face to face, so that our joy may be complete.
13 The children of your elect sister send you their greetings.

There is nothing better than a face-to-face encounter with the people we love! If you're accustomed to communicating through email, you know how easy it can be for words you use to be taken the wrong way. This is especially the case when you're writing about controversial topics or strongly felt convictions. Perhaps a clarifying phone call would help, but you know that a personal meeting would be the best way to ensure that your words are interpreted correctly.

This is how John ended his letter to this unnamed Christian community. He wanted to be with them personally, to share openly with them, to see and hear directly how they were receiving his teaching and his advice. He wanted to be able to read their facial expressions. He wanted them to hear his tone of voice. He didn't want them to miss his most important points and focus on the secondary issues. He knew how important this was, especially when the topic was faith and the Christian life. After all, Christianity is all about communion. It's all about close, intimate relationships, both among believers and with Jesus himself.

John's desire to speak with his readers face to face shows us how important it is that we spend quality time with other Christians. We all need a network of loving and affirming relationships to support and deepen our faith. Whether it is a parish Bible study or small faith-sharing group, whether it is through a separate ecclesial movement such as Cursillo or Focolare, or whether it is through a Third Order affiliated with an order like the Franciscans or Benedictines—no matter where we find it, fellowship is vital to our lives as Christians.

While our need for community with other Christians may seem obvious, we need to recognize how challenging this call can be. We live in a world that prizes individualism and isolation. No matter where we turn, we are encouraged to look out for ourselves, to be our own man or woman, and to prize self-fulfillment above all else. Don't believe it! We all need to live as members of a body, not as isolated individuals. We all need to share our gifts, talents, and spiritual insights with one another. Why? Because it's in fellowship—as brothers and sisters living in unity—that we receive God's choicest blessings (Psalm 133). How much better it is to love each other face to face and share our joy in the Lord with one another in a personal way!

"Father, help me reach out to my brothers and sisters in Christ. Help me build close relationships with other Christians so that I can be a fruitful member of your church. Lord, I want to be one with all your sons and daughters!"

3 John 1-4

[1] The elder to the beloved Gaius, whom I love in truth.

[2] Beloved, I pray that all may go well with you and that you may be in good health, just as it is well with your soul. [3]I was overjoyed when some of the friends arrived and testified to your faithfulness to the truth, namely how you walk in the truth. [4]I have no greater joy than this, to hear that my children are walking in the truth.

This letter may well be the most personal and loving book of the Bible. In it, the presbyter John writes to a single person, Gaius, who is most likely the member of a home church in a neighboring Christian community. The friendship between these two men, founded in their bond in the Lord, is obvious right from the start of this short note. John calls Gaius "beloved," and someone whom he loves "in truth." This is a relationship founded on Christ, not on a common interest in sports or on the fact that their children go to the same school. This is a relationship that both men forged together for the sake of the church and for their own growth in holiness. This, in other words, is fellowship at its finest.

Of course God calls us to love all people, but we will all find ourselves drawn to some people more than to others—especially to those who help support and deepen our walk with the Lord. Even Jesus had closer relationships with certain people. Think about his closest disciples, Peter, James, and John. And what about Mary and Martha and their brother Lazarus? Relationships like these are gifts from God and are very helpful in giving us reflections of God's love and care for us.

St. Aelred of Rievaulx (1110–1167) was an English Cistercian abbot and a wonderful spiritual writer, especially regarding love and charity. His most famous work is called On Spiritual Friendship, and in it Aelred explores and explains aspects of close, personal Christian relationships that we can have with others. Listen to Aelred as he describes Christian friendship:

> A friend is called a guardian of love, or as some would have it, a guardian of the spirit itself. Since it is fitting that my friend be a guardian of our mutual love or the guardian of my own spirit so as to preserve all its secrets in faithful silence, let him, as far as he can, cure and endure such defects as he may observe in it; let him rejoice with his friend in his joys and weep with him in sorrows and feel as his own all that his friend experiences. Friendship, therefore, is that virtue by which spirits are bound by ties of love and sweetness and out of many are made one.

How fortunate are those who have found such friendships in the Lord! If you do, give thanks! If not, ask the Lord to provide them for you. He is your closest friend, and he will surely answer your prayers.

"Lord Jesus, thank you for the gift and promise of Christian friendships. Help me to be, like you, a friend to all and a close friend to many."

3 John 5-8

[5] Beloved, you do faithfully whatever you do for the friends, even though they are strangers to you; [6]they have testified to your love before the church. You will do well to send them on in a manner worthy of God; [7]for they began their journey for the sake of Christ, accepting no support from non-believers. [8]Therefore we ought to support such people, so that we may become co-workers with the truth.

The New Testament letters provide glimpses of the life of the early church. In them we see the gospel being applied to real problems of real men and women as they followed Jesus. The Third Letter of John addressed a conflict over the proper hospitality to be shown to traveling missionaries. An earlier letter had made it clear that the Johannine community should not receive any preacher who distorted the gospel (2 John 10). Now, however, some members of the community (led by one Diotrephes) refused to show hospitality to any missionaries, regardless of doctrine or credentials.

The author condemned this practice as contrary to the gospel. He commended those like Gaius (perhaps a church elder) who still welcomed "strangers" who testified to the truth (3 John 5). By so doing, they were helping to spread the legitimate teaching of those who journeyed for the sake of Christ. During the first two centuries of the church, the gospel was carried to different places by traveling evangelists and teachers. In many cases, these itinerant preachers depended on the hospitality provided by fellow Christians in already-established churches.

Here, in this brief letter, we see God's love lived out. Having heard the gospel and believed in it, this church now shared fellowship with all believers through their union in the Holy Spirit. True, there were difficulties in their attempts to show hospitality, and some abused the call to love. At the same time, however, this brief letter illustrates the principle that believers who support missionaries become "fellow workers in the truth" (3 John 8).

What was true in the church's first centuries remains true today. Even now, we are called to obey the command that "those who love God must love their brothers and sisters also" (1 John 4:21). Do we find it a burden to reach out and care for others? Do we sense an initial reluctance to support the work of the church with our time or resources? Let us ask the Lord to shower his love on us in such a way that we will be moved to love more deeply and thus witness to the power of the gospel to change lives.

"Lord, heal the wounds that make it hard for us to receive your love, and remove the obstacles that keep us from loving each other. Help us to live in unity with all your people until you come again in glory."

3 John 9-15

[9] I have written something to the church; but Diotrephes, who likes to put himself first, does not acknowledge our authority. [10]So if I come, I will call attention to what he is doing in spreading false charges against us. And not content with those charges, he refuses to welcome the friends, and even prevents those who want to do so and expels them from the church.

[11] Beloved, do not imitate what is evil but imitate what is good. Whoever does good is from God; whoever does evil has not seen God. [12]Everyone has testified favorably about Demetrius, and so has the truth itself. We also testify for him, and you know that our testimony is true.

[13] I have much to write to you, but I would rather not write with pen and ink; [14]instead I hope to see you soon, and we will talk together face to face.

[15] Peace to you. The friends send you their greetings. Greet the friends there, each by name.

Whoever does good is from God; whoever does what is evil
has not seen God. (3 John 11)

This passage should remind us of a similar theme that was used near the beginning of 1 John: "God is light, and in him there is no darkness at all" (1 John 1:5). John uses the metaphor of light to mean truth and goodness, and he uses darkness to mean false-hood and evil. Thus, when we do good, we imitate God who is good.

For John, to "do good" is to live and act according to the teaching handed on to us by Jesus and the apostles. It is to seek and uphold the goodness of God in every situation. As Christians, we are called to overcome evil with good (Romans 12:21), and we know this is not an impossible calling, because God can bring good out of every situation, even those that appear evil.

Have you ever looked for specific opportunities to do good? Are there trying situations at your workplace where tension is high or ill will has the upper hand? Is it possible that a kind word or two from you can help defuse the situation? You don't even have to talk about Jesus or the gospel. Just by being a peaceful or encouraging presence at work, you can change the atmosphere and create an environment of openness to God. The same goes for family difficulties or argu-ments and for tension between neighbors or friends.

Jesus said, "Let your light shine before others, so that they may see your good works and give glory to your Father in heaven" (Matthew 5:16). This is the beginning of evangelization to others, and an essen-tial step on the path of holiness for ourselves. It is not always easy. It is not always enjoyable. But the fruits are well worth the effort. So let us strive to do good each day, so that our Father in heaven may be glori-fied and so that others may come to see him reflected in our lives.

"Lord Jesus, help me to seek opportunities each day to do good and help others. May your light shine in me, O Lord, that others may be drawn to you and come to embrace you themselves."

A Vote of Confidence

The Letter of Jude

A VOTE OF CONFIDENCE

A Vote of Confidence
An Introduction to the Letter of Jude

Leo Zanchettin

Sandwiched between the letters of John and the Book of Revelation is a short epistle that is one of the least read of all the New Testament letters. Bearing the name of Jude, "servant of Jesus Christ and brother of James" (verse 1), this letter can be easily overlooked as we move from the intimacy of the epistles of John to the majesty and drama of Revelation. And if we do pause to read it, we encounter a world filled with images and allusions that are quite foreign to us: stories and legends taken from obscure Jewish writings from the decades just before and after Christ. But if we take the time to wade through its images and arguments, the Letter of Jude offers us a Spirit-filled perspective on how to hold fast to the Lord in times of confusion, as well as how to build up the church no matter what challenges we are facing.

Who Was Jude? From its opening verses, it is clear that this letter will raise more questions than it answers. While we are familiar with the names associated with the other New Testament letters—John, Peter, Paul, and James—we really don't know much about Jude. He is named in the gospels as a "brother" of Jesus (along with James and Joseph/Joses and Simon—Matthew 13:55; Mark 6:3), but nothing else is said about him. Was he one of Joseph's children from a previous marriage? Was he a cousin of Jesus'? Often linked with the James who was head of the church in Jerusalem (Acts 12:17; 15:13; Galatians 1:19), that Jude may well have been an influential figure among Jewish Christians in Palestine. These believers embraced the gospel but also held on to their Jewish identity with deep devotion.

But if we assume that this letter was written by a close relative of Jesus', a problem arises as soon as we read past the first verse and get into the body of the letter. If the author knew Jesus personally, we might expect him to say something about Jesus' life or ministry. But at no point does the author give us any insights into Jesus' personality or tell us anything particular about his teaching. In fact, at no point does Jesus of Nazareth come into the picture at all—only the risen Lord, who will come at the end of time to judge the living and the dead.

Instead of talking about Jesus' own ministry, the author asks his readers to remember what the *apostles* taught, and to reverence the faith that was handed down to them—presumably by other, more direct, eyewitnesses to the life of Christ (verses 17, 3). Statements like these hint at a setting at least one generation removed from the time of the apostles, leading some scholars to conclude that Jude was written near the end of the first century, after most of the first generation of Christians had already died. Thus, it is possible that the author wrote in the name of Jude in order to give his words a greater sense of authority—a common practice in the world of ancient Greece and Rome.

A Jewish Christian Source. Where did the Letter of Jude come from? And to whom was it written? Most likely this epistle was composed in Palestine and was intended for a Jewish Christian audience. The figure of Jude seems not to have been very well known outside of Jesus' ancestral home of Galilee. His connection with James could have gained him some positive notoriety in Judea, but that's about as far as his name seems to have traveled. He is not mentioned in Acts or in Paul's letters—all of which are focused on the gentile lands to the west of Jerusalem. Moreover, the Letter of Jude is filled with references to Jewish literature that would have circulated widely within Palestine but not much farther.

We also know that a vibrant Jewish Christian community associated with James, "the brother of the Lord," existed in Palestine during
the decades before and after the destruction of the Temple in A.D. 70.
This community produced variations on the four gospels and could
well have produced its own epistles. It is also conceivable that this
community faced some of the threats and challenges that the Letter
of Jude addresses. Sadly, however, the community seems not to have
survived in Palestine very long after the final Jewish rebellion against
Rome in A.D. 135. Some members fled to Syria, and others to Egypt,
but precious little of their literature has been passed down, and our
information on them after 135 is sketchy at best. It is quite possible,
however, that Jude arose from within this environment, thus opening a window on a world that was largely overlooked as the church
became increasingly gentile.

Beware the Impostors! One curious aspect of this letter is the reason
it was written in the first place. The author tells his readers that he had
intended to write a more comprehensive letter "about the salvation
we share," but that he found it necessary instead to write a brief and
passionate appeal urging them to "contend for the faith" (verse 3).
Evidently, certain unnamed "intruders" had infiltrated their church
and were trying to "pervert the grace of our God into licentiousness"
(verse 4). So rather than give a more comprehensive view of the gospel, the author felt compelled to write a somewhat hurried note of
warning and exhortation. He wanted to help his readers steer clear of
these intruders' false teachings—particularly the way they were advo-
cating immorality in the name of Christian freedom.

What follows from this initial warning, then, is a series of remind-
ers from both the Old Testament and from popular Jewish writings
about the fate of those who either grumbled against the Lord or who
turned away from their covenant with God. The author talks about
the Israelites who rebelled against Yahweh during their desert journey

to the promised land and were punished for it (verses 5-6). He mentions the people of Sodom and Gomorrah, whose immorality was legendary, and who threatened even the angels who had come to rescue Lot (verse 7). Cain, Korah, and Balaam are also given as examples of rebels who met their doom at the hand of the Lord (verse 11).

The author draws as well from the world of Jewish apocalyptic literature, quoting writings such as the Testament of the Twelve Patriarchs, the Book of Enoch, and the Assumption of Moses (verses 8-9, 14-16) to show that those who contend against God will find not freedom but judgment, not praise but condemnation. As far as Jude is concerned, the people who were infiltrating the church are just as wicked as these notorious enemies of righteousness—and they are guaranteed to meet a similar end.

"But You . . . " This wide-ranging rogues' gallery is impressive indeed, and it is easy to see how a modern-day reader might miss the "forest" of the letter's argument for the "trees" of all the villains. But at its heart, the Letter of Jude is an exhortation to beleaguered disciples struggling to sort truth from lies and fighting against the temptations that naturally accompany false teachings.

It is not until Jude has finished with his examples of past miscreants that he gets to the heart of his letter: he reminds his readers of who they are in Christ and calls them to live in the power of the Holy Spirit, whom they received at baptism (verses 17-23). *But you*, he writes, are not like these false Christians. You know the difference between flesh and spirit, because you have experienced the Spirit's power in your life; you know the difference between the truth and lies, because you have already embraced the gospel handed down by the apostles. And since you know these things, you are quite capable of praying in the Spirit and of having compassion and mercy on those whose faith is wavering. You are more than able to contend for the faith into which you are baptized and by which you have been redeemed. *You don't have to give in to these impostors!*

So ultimately, despite the dark tone of its middle section, the Letter of Jude is filled with confidence. The author closes by telling his readers that he is convinced that God can bring them safely to heaven despite the challenges they are now facing. God is more than capable of keeping them from "falling" and of making them "stand without blemish in the presence of his glory" (verse 24).

He Will Keep You Safe. It is very encouraging that Jude doesn't threaten his readers at all. He doesn't cajole them to obedience or bully them into complying with his requests. He simply points out the difference between being in the darkness of sin, as exemplified by figures from Israel's past, and being in the light of God's salvation, which is their situation. He knows that if they simply walk in that light, nothing can overcome them.

And so, confident in his readers' clarity and even more confident in the power of God, Jude closes his letter not by issuing another warning but by singing a hymn of praise to the God who has chosen and saved his people—and who will keep them safe until eternal life.

A Vote of Confidence

Jude 1-4

¹ Jude, a servant of Jesus Christ and brother of James,
To those who are called, who are beloved in God the Father and
kept safe for Jesus Christ:
² May mercy, peace, and love be yours in abundance.
³ Beloved, while eagerly preparing to write to you about the salvation we share, I find it necessary to write and appeal to you to contend for the faith that was once for all entrusted to the saints. ⁴For
certain intruders have stolen in among you, people who long ago
were designated for this condemnation as ungodly, who pervert the
grace of our God into licentiousness and deny our only Master and
Lord, Jesus Christ. ⁊

There's no shortage of advice these days about how we should
live our lives. But how do we know what is good advice and
what isn't? The Letter of Jude was written to a community
that faced the same problem. It's advice applies as much to us as it did
to them: follow the teachings of the gospel.

Jude identifies himself as "the brother of James," most likely the
James who was the leader of the Jerusalem church in its earliest years
(Acts 15:12-19; 1 Corinthians 15:7; Galatians 1:18-19). He writes
the letter with the express purpose of encouraging his readers to
"contend" for their faith because of some "intruders" who are causing
problems. Although he never specifically identifies the people he is
warning about or the exact nature of their errors, Jude does give a
clear warning to these early Christians and gives many examples to
show that God will judge those who rebel against the gospel as well
as those who cause trouble for the faithful people of God.

Throughout the history of the church, there have been people
who have distorted the Christian faith that has been handed down

to us from the apostles. We don't have to look very far in our day to find contemporary distortions of the gospel. Some claim that Jesus was not really God. Others say that there is no sin and so no need for redemption. Still others try to teach that we are so hopelessly sinful that we can never hope to experience God's love, that all we can do is pray that somehow we will squeeze into heaven. And yet in the midst of all the confusion, deception, and false teachings, the light of the gospel continues to shine. All we need to do is let this light shine in our hearts, and we too will become beacons of truth and holiness.

We're fortunate to have the *Catechism of the Catholic Church* as a resource if we ever have questions about what are true teachings of the church and what aren't. Why not devote the next few weeks to studying some aspect of your faith as it is presented in the *Catechism?* Perhaps you can even do this with some friends in your parish who want to learn more as well. Such group study, discussion, and prayer can go a long way in strengthening your faith and drawing you closer to the Lord. And, as an added benefit, it will help you share your faith with others.

"Jesus, help me to know the faith that has come down to me from the apostles, the faith that the church has always taught. Thank you for the precious gift of your gospel message. Come, Spirit, and fill my heart with a greater love for all that is good and holy and true!"

Jude 5-13

[5] Now I desire to remind you, though you are fully informed, that the Lord, who once for all saved a people out of the land of Egypt, afterward destroyed those who did not believe. [6]And the angels who did not keep their own position, but left their proper dwelling, he has kept in eternal chains in deepest darkness for the judgment of the

great day. ⁷Likewise, Sodom and Gomorrah and the surrounding cities, which, in the same manner as they, indulged in sexual immorality and pursued unnatural lust, serve as an example by undergoing a punishment of eternal fire.

⁸ Yet in the same way these dreamers also defile the flesh, reject authority, and slander the glorious ones. ⁹But when the archangel Michael contended with the devil and disputed about the body of Moses, he did not dare to bring a condemnation of slander against him, but said, "The Lord rebuke you!" ¹⁰But these people slander whatever they do not understand, and they are destroyed by those things that, like irrational animals, they know by instinct. ¹¹Woe to them! For they go the way of Cain, and abandon themselves to Balaam's error for the sake of gain, and perish in Korah's rebellion. ¹²These are blemishes on your love-feasts, while they feast with you without fear, feeding themselves. They are waterless clouds carried along by the winds; autumn trees without fruit, twice dead, uprooted; ¹³wild waves of the sea, casting up the foam of their own shame; wandering stars, for whom the deepest darkness has been reserved forever.

As he warns his readers against those who would distort the gospel, Jude gives several examples from Israel's past of those who rebelled against God and the moral life to which he calls us. Some of the stories he uses come from the apocryphal books of 1 Enoch (verse 6) and the Assumption of Moses (verse 9). Others come from Jewish oral traditions that go beyond the stories recorded in the Bible. And while we may be inclined to dismiss these accounts because of their sources, the Letter of Jude itself is part of the inspired Scripture, and its teachings are authentic and worthy of our prayer and acceptance.

Let's face it. Rebellion against God is part of our fallen nature. It's something we will have to contend with all of our lives. But that doesn't mean that we have to give in. Quite the opposite! God has given us his Holy Spirit for just this purpose: to strengthen us and to help us lead a life pleasing to him. Through the Spirit, we can overcome temptation; we can surrender our hearts and minds to the Lord; and we can become increasingly more holy.

So how do we nourish the life of grace and our submission to the Holy Spirit? The answers are always the same: through daily prayer; through immersion in the Scriptures; through fellowship with other committed Christians; and through the grace, power, and consolation that flow from the sacramental life of the church. All of these ingredients work together to train us and to help keep our eyes on Jesus throughout the day.

But what do we do when, despite our best efforts, we still find ourselves resisting or even rebelling against the Lord and his will for us? First, we need to acknowledge the truth that this is what we are doing. Then, we need to confess our sin and seek the cleansing power of his mercy. And finally, we should ask God to strengthen us, even as we firmly resolve to follow him more closely in the future. The good news is that Jesus has shed his blood to win our forgiveness and has sent the Holy Spirit to help us live a life worthy of our calling.

We all sin and fall short of the glory of God (Romans 3:23); yet, through the great love of the Lord, we can all return to the Father and "approach the throne of grace with boldness, so that we may receive mercy and find grace to help in time of need" (Hebrews 4:16).

"Father, forgive me when I resist your plan for my life and even rebel against you. Thank you for helping me through your Son, Jesus Christ, and through the gift of the Holy Spirit."

Jude 14-16

¹⁴ It was also about these that Enoch, in the seventh generation from Adam, prophesied, saying, "See, the Lord is coming with ten thousands of his holy ones, ¹⁵to execute judgment on all, and to convict everyone of all the deeds of ungodliness that they have committed in such an ungodly way, and of all the harsh things that ungodly sinners have spoken against him." ¹⁶These are grumblers and malcontents; they indulge their own lusts; they are bombastic in speech, flattering people to their own advantage. ⌒

Again, Jude uses Jewish tradition contained in passages outside of the Bible to remind his readers that it had been foretold that the "ungodly" would come among God's people. Jude's underlying message is that God alone will judge them. Although these people might be very active and outspoken, causing disturbances to the Christians of Jude's time, God will ultimately deal with them.

Sometimes, in our zeal for God and his ways, we may want to take things into our own hands and deal with people in the church whom we think are troublemakers. The trouble is, when we take matters in our own hands, we tend to take them out of God's hands—sometimes with disastrous results! In these cases, it is better to recall Jude's counsel in this letter: God will ultimately deal with them. And he will do it far better than we could: he will lead them to repentance and a change of heart!

So what should we do when we believe that certain "ungodly" people are causing harm to the faith and disturbing the life and practice of the faithful? First, we need to make sure that we are not doing the same! Remember that Jesus cautioned us against trying to remove a speck from a brother's eye while a log remained in our own eye. So the first step is to ask God to open our eyes to our own

181

lives and show us where we need to repent for any ways we might be disrupting or disturbing our brothers and sisters in Christ. After we have examined our own hearts, we can then pray for anyone that we believe is truly causing harm. We may even want to speak with that person, if appropriate—but always in humility and love. We can also share our concerns with our pastor.

As Jude will counsel in the following verses of his letter, our main task in such cases is to continue to grow in our faith and grow closer to Jesus with the help of the Holy Spirit. If we can keep these goals in the forefront of our hearts, we will find it far easier to understand how we should respond. So always put love first. Always hold to the humility and gentleness of Christ. That's the best way to not only contend for the faith but also protect it.

"Father, help me to be a source of encouragement, wisdom, and guidance to those you have placed in my path. May I always seek to speak your truth in love, patience, and humility."

Jude 17-25

[17] But you, beloved, must remember the predictions of the apostles of our Lord Jesus Christ; [18]for they said to you, "In the last time there will be scoffers, indulging their own ungodly lusts." [19]It is these worldly people, devoid of the Spirit, who are causing divisions. [20]But you, beloved, build yourselves up on your most holy faith; pray in the Holy Spirit; [21]keep yourselves in the love of God; look forward to the mercy of our Lord Jesus Christ that leads to eternal life. [22]And have mercy on some who are wavering; [23]save others by snatching them out of the fire; and have mercy on still others with fear, hating even the tunic defiled by their bodies.

[24] Now to him who is able to keep you from falling, and to make

you stand without blemish in the presence of his glory with rejoic-
ing, ²⁵to the only God our Savior, through Jesus Christ our Lord, be
glory, majesty, power, and authority, before all time and now and
forever. Amen. ✑

Keep yourselves in the love of God. (Jude 21)

What does it mean to keep ourselves in God's love? More
than just "feeling" that God loves us, this command
encompasses the ways we use memory. We may experience
feelings of joy and happiness when we pray, but feelings can fade, and
difficult times can cloud our emotions and threaten our peace. However, as we recall God's faithfulness to us in the past, we will begin to
rely on God more and to trust in him even in the darkest of times.

Throughout Scripture, God calls us to remember his great deeds
and his steadfast love. He instituted the feast of Passover as a time
for the Israelites to recall their deliverance from slavery (Exodus
12:14). It was an observance to be held year after year so that Jewish
people everywhere would never forget their deliverance from slavery. Similarly, at the Last Supper, Jesus established the Eucharist
as a perpetual memorial of his death and resurrection: "Do this in
remembrance of me" (Luke 22:19).

In addition to such communal acts of recollection, it is also vital
that we remember when and how God has revealed himself to us
personally. Our minds tend to drift away from God (Hebrews 2:1),
and so we must continually pay attention to all he has done for
us and anchor ourselves to his love. What were the circumstances
surrounding those times when God's love and forgiveness filled you
with hope? How did you react? What resolutions did you make?

As Jude suggests, remembering the times when God has manifested his love will help us to remain steadfast in our faith. It is

important to keep our memories clear and active so that we can stand on the truths of the Lord—especially during times of difficulty. Regular and heartfelt worship at Mass and in personal prayer can awaken the memory of God's covenant with us. By nourishing our memories daily, we fill find it increasingly easy to remain in God's love, no matter what situation we are in.

"Lord Jesus, I trust in your mercy and love for me. Help me apply my mind to your truths. I dedicate myself to walking with you throughout the day and to being ready to share my faith with others."